THE DHIKR O
By Dawud Abdur-Rahman

Published by Starry Night Publishing.Com
Rochester, New York

Copyright 2012 Dawud Abdur-Rahman

Dawud Abdur-Rahman

Table of Contents

Dawud Abdur-Rahman

Acknowledgements

All Praise is due to Allah, The All Knowing (Al-Alim) who bestows knowledge, and who rewards without measure those that strive and study to gain some insight into the workings of His Creation.

This humble effort would not have been possible without the support of many people, first and foremost my loving wife Monica. My children Jasmine, Andrew and Alia are a constant source of pride and joy. My mother Willie Mae Ward has always been an inspiration for me. I can't thank enough my family, friends and colleagues for their continued love and encouragement. Thanks to my brother in law Leonard Gilbert; he was every bit a big brother to me as I was growing up. I deeply appreciate the continued support and friendship of the Islamic Society of Southern Prince George's County. I would like to acknowledge the early encouragement of Ibrahim El-Hibri. A special shout out goes to my good friends and Brothers in Al-Islam, Abu Mubarak, Khalil Shadeed and Bilal Hassan; who with many others, nudged me down this leg of my journey.

The Dhikr of Authenticity

Whoever you are...**BE IT!**

Whatever good inspires you....**STRIVE FOR IT!**

RESPOND to the Call to Life;

    With a Humble Certainty;

        Grounded in Love and a Reasoning Faith;

            Reinforced by the Peace of a Patient
Steadfastness;

                And Preserved by a Vigilant
Consciousness of Allah and
Creation

Āmīn

Dawud Abdur-Rahman

The Dhikr of Authenticity
The Essay

<u>Introduction</u>

The "Dhikr[1] of Authenticity" is a prologue to what I pray will be a series of publications on my observations and thoughts on Al-Islam[2]. This prologue evolved out of a larger project I have been working on periodically for several years entitled "The Next Wave, Black[3] American Muslims at the Intersection of Destiny and Opportunity".

Many of the concepts and ideas that I intend, by the Grace of Allah[4], to explore in more detail in future efforts are introduced in this work. Except where noted, I use the Saheeh International translation of the Holy Qur'an, as this is my preferred Qur'an translation. I have found this to be an accurate translation of the Arabic Qur'an that has minimal and clearly identified clarifications from the translator.

I believe the particular experience of any people must necessarily inform that people's authentic expression of Al-Islam. Dr. Cornell West stated that any serious examination of black culture should begin with what W.E.B Dubois dubbed, in Faustian terms the "spiritual strivings" of black people[5]. Accordingly, I frequently reference scholars of Black history, with particular emphasis on W.E.B Dubois,[6] a personal favorite due to his long legacy of scholarship, reasoned spirituality and uncompromising commitment to finding a comprehensive solution to Negro problems[7].

I have heard more than one scholar of Black history say that any serious scholar of this field of study has to wrestle with DuBois at some point. I consider his writings and analysis a viable and valuable baseline for discussions of root issues and causes of problems still plaguing, by varying degrees, the Black community.

Given that historical linkages to African Islam are more romantic than factual for most Black Americans, I have accepted the view that the most significant period that influenced the development of Black American Islam is rooted in the racist conditions of the early twentieth century; a period that gave rise to an ideological maelstrom of responses to those conditions.

DuBois is preeminent[8] in his analysis of "Souls of Black Folk"[9] during this formulative period as various competing ideologies emerged and synthesized various expressions of Islam[10] with Black Strivings and Black Religion and presented Islam as a viable alternative response to Christianity for Black Identity and liberation ideology[11].

This introductory effort is offered in the spirit of my understanding that there is a diversity of views in the Muslim Ummah including the Black American Muslim community. However, my observation is that more Muslims with different approaches to Al-Islam are beginning to express, in different ways and degrees many of the ideas I express in this work. I see this as an encouraging trend as the work of Islamic revival may be accomplished by a number of groups or individuals[12].

It is my earnest prayer that there can be an increased unity of purpose and direction as we align causes as our consciousness as Muslims in America continues to evolve and mature. Allah has revealed in the Holy Qur'an:

> **2:148** For each [religious following] is a [prayer] direction toward which it faces. So race to [all that is] good. Wherever you may be, Allah will bring you forth [for judgment] all together. Indeed, Allah is over all things competent.

My personal belief is that the Holy Qur'an has a personal message from The Creator[13] to anyone that approaches it with an open heart[14] and mind[15]. One of my initial reactions to the Holy Qur'an when I began studying it almost 20 years ago was that it is a Self Help/ Positive Thinking manual[16] from The Lord[17] of the universe.

The values of self help and personal responsibility were instilled in me in large part by being raised by a single mother in West Philadelphia who managed to raise me, obtain her G.E.D. and eventually go on to graduate college in 1981 with a B.A. in Social Welfare from Temple University four years before I graduated from Temple University's Business School.

There was a time when I was a freshman and my mother was a senior at Temple. Although I was raised by a single mother, I was more fortunate than many inner city boys because I had a relationship with my father growing up. I knew he loved me and he was there when I needed him.

I can still remember going to class with my mother at night sometimes when I was too young to stay at home alone because she could not afford a babysitter. I also remember the many nights she and my sister Mona stayed up late as my sister typed my mother's handwritten and dictated papers as she strove to advance her education.

In my opinion, single mothers who struggle, strive and persevere, cobbling together the resources available to them are often unlettered experts at reconciling faith, life and "rules". They are required to develop a methodology to navigate a potholed road of life. My mother recited the "Serenity Prayer" often:

God, grant me the serenity to accept the things I cannot
change;
Courage to change the things I can;
And wisdom to know the difference[18]

One of the overarching mottos I heard in my house was, "God
helps those that help themselves, if a door is closed, God will
open a window![19]" Anyone that wants to know what needs to
be fixed in any system would be well informed to include a
panel of single mothers. I realized as I was writing this book
that the sense of a striving, practical faith from my early life
experience underlies "The Dhikr of Authenticity."

I believe the experience of Black Strivings in America is
integral to inform our understanding and participation in the
conversation regarding the development of Al-Islam. The
overwhelming majority of Arabic words have a root, which is
generally three consonants interlinked with vowels. This root
provides the basic lexical meaning of the word.[20]

The word Islam is derived from the Arabic root S-L-M which
means, among other things, peace, purity, submission and
obedience. In the religious sense the word Islam means
submission to the Will of God and obedience to His law[21]. I
believe the temporal struggle of that submission is to live life in
accordance with the will of Allah. The discourse around that
struggle implicitly or explicitly includes a discussion on Sharia
as Sharia, which is philosophically speaking the methodology
to live in accordance with the will of Allah[22].

In *The Spirit of Islamic Law*, Professor Bernard G. Weiss
states "In archaic Arabic, the term shar'a means 'path to the
water hole. When we consider the importance of a well-
trodden path to a source of water for man and beast in the arid
desert environment, we can readily appreciate why this term in
Muslim usage should have become a metaphor for a whole
way of life ordained by God."[23]

Accordingly, I have come to understand that surrendering to Allah is to find your path to life. DuBois argued that the principal defining characteristic, mission, and message of a people is the cultural expression of the shared struggle for survival[24]. I see this cultural or ethnic expression as the true religion of a people; it may or may not be consistent with the professed "religious" beliefs of a people.

In my view, the Black experience has been an incubator for many of the challenges confronting the Muslim world with regard to the development of Al-Islam. Many scholars and lay people in the Muslim world are struggling today to develop a methodology to understand Al-Islam in a modern context. Among the approaches under consideration is a focus on higher purposes and intents of the revelation of the Qur'an and mission of the Prophet Muhammad (PBUH[25]). Specific issues generating critical interest include the spiritual and intellectual equality of women and the status of religious minorities. Matriculation through the Black experience includes daily and historical lessons in these critical areas.

Black Americans have a distinguished history of identifying and championing the higher intents and purposes of the laws of God and men. After all, Black Americans embraced and championed the values of Christianity as well as America's founding principles even as the Bible and United States Constitution were used for centuries to justify our enslavement and perpetual disenfranchisement.

It was not an uncommon occurrence after the heinous attacks on the World Trade Center on September 11, 2001 for Black American Muslims to analogously explain to family members, friends and co-workers the warped understanding of the "Islam" by terrorists as analogous to the warped "Christianity" and hypocritical application of America's professed values by White Supremacists to Blacks during America's slavery and Jim Crow eras[26].

13

The ability to discern the true underlying values of any professed belief system is an important aptitude inherently developed in Black culture and history that are now lacking in large parts of the Muslim world as it struggles to reconcile Al-Islam, specific cultures and modernity. These qualities should not be lost by Black American Muslims as the application of Al-Islam to Black Strivings continues to evolve.

This book is written from my particular Black American Muslim perspective not because it is written only for Muslims in America (or anywhere else) of African descent, but because the Qur'an was revealed, the Prophet Muhammad (PBUH) lived and Al-Islam is always implemented within a specific cultural context.[27]   Therefore, my culture, and personal history, like all other Muslim people has influenced my understanding of Al-Islam[28].

Whether an author or scholar is conscious of it or not, I believe most, if not all perspectives on Al-Islam are written from a particular cultural perspective; and that should be expected. In the same way that we can often learn lessons from particular stories from specific families and cultures, and we do learn from them, in the same way this book is written from that spirit. The challenge is to avoid reading *into* the revelation[29] as opposed to deriving an authentic application of Al-Islam calibrated by time, place and circumstance (see figure 1).

Accordingly, I offer this contribution as a companion to the many efforts currently underway in masajid, academia, stage and during everyday conversations and interactions with family, friends and colleagues by many sincere Believers across the rich diversity of communities in the ummah to reconcile Al-Islam with our contemporary life.

I pray that Allah blesses me for the best of my intentions and forgive any errors as I undertake this part of my personal journey along the paths of Allah.

> **29:69** And those who strive for Us – We will surely guide them to Our ways. And indeed, Allah is with the doers of good.

Dawud Abdur-Rahman

Allah and Family First

The Dhikr itself evolved out of an expression I've gotten into the habit of using fairly often when I talk to my children. That is, "Whoever you are...**BE IT**".

What my wife and I, and I think most parents try to do is to reinforce our children's inherent self worth, uniqueness and to encourage them to explore areas that seem interesting to them and through which they can find fulfillment to be true to and express themselves. As parents, we try to instill values and guidelines that we have come to believe will help our children achieve fulfillment.

I am among those that believe that the first most fundamental unit of any society is families and that preparing our children to be responsible, socially conscious adults is the key activity that each of us contributes to a healthy society. This is consistent with one of my favorite ayah[30] in the Holy Qur'an:

> **66:6**   O you who have believed, protect yourselves and your families from a Fire whose fuel is people and stones, over which are [appointed] angels, harsh and severe; they do not disobey Allah in what He commands them but do what they are commanded.

I believe that the quest to find your path to spiritual fulfillment, all the while, remaining meaningfully engaged with family, friends and larger community is the perennially noble human endeavor.   This is consistent with admonitions in the Qur'an and Sunnah[31] of the Prophet Muhammad (PBUH) regarding asceticism[32] [33].

There are inevitable ups and downs during your journey. Intentionally striving to live a humbly, prayerful life where you attempt to rise above pettiness and base desires while seeking to help others, simple as this may seem, sometimes places a person that is striving to live this way in a position as a role model or a leader[34]. The Prophet Muhammad (PBUH) has advised that actions are judged by intentions and that we are all leaders on some level. The Prophet has advised:

> "Everyone of you is a guardian and is responsible for his charge; the ruler is a guardian and is responsible for his subjects; the man is a guardian in his family and responsible for his charges; a woman is a guardian of her husband's house and responsible for her charges; and the servant is a guardian of his master's property and is responsible for his charge. A man is a guardian of his father's property and responsible for his charges; so every one of you is a guardian and responsible for his charges." [35]

Anybody that finds themselves in a leadership position must accept the fact that whether a person sought to be a role model or not, the reality is that leadership, whether formal or informal carries with it a sacred trust that requires constant self vigilance to preserve the integrity of the trust.

The methodology I have chosen to find spiritual fulfillment is the path of Al-Islam. I concede that the term "spiritual" means many things to many people[36] and can be elusive. My personal definition of spirituality is "values embraced as result of acknowledgement of a higher power or reality".

I don't think of spirituality as a necessarily complicated, mystically distant concept but rather as a conscious striving to manifest the most good in every action, interaction and relationship possible.   I have always thought of spirituality as transcending religion. Spirituality is the underlying principles that   religious practices are supposed to induce[37].

I understand spirituality as a synthesis of the Qur'anic concepts of Dhikr and Al-Ihsan. Dhikr meaning Remembrance and Al-Ihsan, The Good, described by the Prophet Muhammad (PBUH) as "worshipping Allah as if you see Allah, because he most certainly sees you[38]." From an Islamic perspective, all of our activities are Ibadah[39], worship when understood within the singularly important Islamic concept of Tauheed.

For Muslims Allah, the proper name applied to the Being who exists necessarily, by Himself[40] occupies the central position in every Muslim place, every Muslim action, every Muslim thought. The presence of Allah fills the Muslim consciousness at all times. With the Muslim, Allah is indeed a sublime obsession[41]. Allah is the name used by any Arabic speaking person when referring to the One and Only God.

Because the Islamic concept of Ibadah, worship, is inclusive of all activities. I don't focus on rituals exclusively as the means to produce some metaphysical experience, but rather to teach, remind and reinforce values like honesty, fairness, compassion, forgiveness and patience that you bring to every situation as Allah has revealed:

> **2:152** So remember Me; I will remember you. And be grateful to Me and do not deny Me.

> **55:60** Is there any Reward for Good [Al-Ihsan] other than Good [Al-Ihsan]?

> **2:177** Righteousness is not that you turn your faces toward the east or the west, but [true] righteousness is [in] one who believes in Allah, the Last Day, the angels, the Book, and the prophets and gives wealth, in spite of love for it, to relatives, orphans, the needy, the traveler, those who ask [for help], and for freeing slaves; [and who] establishes prayer and gives zakah; [those who] fulfill their promise when they promise; and [those who] are patient in poverty and hardship and during battle.

Those are the ones who have been true, and it is those who are the righteous.

I count myself among those people Allah, in the Holy Qur'an called Muslim[42]; those that are struggling to submit to the Will of Allah as expressed in the Holy Qur'an and authentic Sunnah of the Prophet Muhammad (PBUH). This is the path someone begins to embark upon after taking a declaration of faith, the Shahada. To declare that there is no object of worship except Allah and that the Prophet Muhammad ibn Abdullah (May Allah's peace and blessings be upon him) is his Servant and Messenger is to confirm your identity as a Muslim.

To profess and to believe on all levels of consciousness and by the grace of Allah, sub-consciousness that there is no object of worship except Allah and to further believe that Allah is the Lord, Creator, Evolver of all creation without exception or qualification is to orient your entire conscious and unconscious psyche with the concept of Tauheed, Oneness. To believe that there is One God, One Humanity, One Creation and that every aspect of the creation, including yourself is a sign of Allah[43] puts you in a healthy starting place to commence a spiritual, primarily inner journey to draw nearer[44] to Allah by shedding those aspects of your psyche and physical life that distance you from Allah.

If I can be so bold to appropriate a title of honor used by the Shia[45], we are all ayatollahs[46], an Arabic word meaning Sign of Allah. We are all signs of Allah[47] in our creation and being, we all have a purpose. The Prophet Muhammad (PBUH) is reported to have said that the Greater Jihad is the struggle against your baser self.[48] In my mind, that baser self can be that internal voice that keeps telling you that somehow, by your creation and being, you are less worthy, less good, less smart, less attractive and not deserving of everything that Allah has made available to you by your faith, choices and striving.[49]

The Dhikr of Authenticity summarizes my understanding of the starting point for the manifestation of Tauheed on a comprehensively personal level. The struggle to know yourself and to realize your potential by engaging in the inner jihad to understand and appreciate Allah and those aspects of yourself that Allah, by his will has created in you is a part of the inner journey. Allah has revealed in the Holy Qur'an:

> **64:3**. He created the heavens and earth in truth and formed you and perfected your forms; and to Him is the [final] destination.
> **64: 4**. He knows what is within the heavens and earth and knows what you conceal and what you declare. And Allah is Knowing of that within the breasts.
>
> **14:7** And [remember] when your Lord proclaimed, 'If you are grateful, I will surely increase you [in favor]; but if you deny, indeed, My punishment is severe.' " .

Certainly, not liking yourself, not appreciating your uniqueness, denying or being ashamed of your experience, family and tradition can only create a sense of an inner dissonance, or a kind of double consciousness[50] as W.E.B. DuBois conceived it that will not result in a peaceful, secure sense of self. Further, denying the signs of Allah is disbelief[51]. The term Muslim in the Arabic language is derived from the root letters that that are equivalent to the English letters s-l-m (salama). The base meaning is "to be safe and sound"[52]. To be a Muslim then is to be a person that professes the desire to strive to be safe, sound, secure and at peace within themselves and then to strive to extend that peace to their environment. Dissonance is the opposite of Al-Islam.

Dawud Abdur-Rahman

Context

At the same time the Dhikr of Authenticity is a product of my personal inner jihad and the desire to be the best person I can be, I am conscious of the current environment of the Muslim world generally and particularly, the Black American Muslim experience. When one considers the status of the Black American Islamic experience, it could be argued that there has never been a time when the moment is so ripe with anticipation of the next step in the process of Islamization in the Black American Muslim community. When one considers:

1. A new Generation of leaders is emerging all over America and the world; the leadership of the Black American Muslim Community is no different;
2. There is concern in the Muslim community, and particularly in the Black American Muslim community about the appropriate strategies to address the needs of young people;
3. Various communities are engaged in formulating a "next step" in the evolving story of the Black American Muslim experience, though there does not appear to be a consensus across communities and sometimes within communities about exactly what that step should be;
4. This is all happening at a time when the once romantic (and never correct) notion of Al-Islam as the silver bullet for solving issues of racism, identity and historical/ cultural connection to the "Mother Land" have ebbed;
5. We live in a multicultural reality where simple labels are insufficient to chart a path[53]. The world we live in is much more complicated than the simple divisions of belief vs. unbelief or Black vs. White[54];

Now more than ever, as Black American Muslims continue along the path to draw nearer to Allah a critical and objective analysis of our goals and those of others needs to be laid bare so that valid understandings of the Qur'an and Sunnah of the Prophet Muhammad (PBUH) considering appropriate contexts — time, place and circumstance — can be implemented.

In Robert Dannin's book, "Black Pilgrimage to Islam" he states, "In the 14 centuries since the Prophet Muhammad (PBUH) lived, Islam has radiated from its center of origin on the Arabia peninsula to Africa, Asia Minor, Europe, and further into Asia by various means, including military conquest, political, commercial and cultural hegemony. African-Americans have sought out and devised a unique path to this religion."[55]   This should not be at all surprising given the uniqueness of the Black American experience.

Further, the Qur'an, Sunnah and Islamic history suggest that an authentic Islamic expression develops out of any people's distinct cultural and historical experience.   The Prophet Muhammad (PBUH) is reported to have said, "Those who were best in the pre-Islamic period, are the best in Islam, if they comprehend (the religious knowledge)."[56]

According to Islamic scholar Dr. Sherman Jackson, from the time of the Third Resurrection[57] and the basis of Islamic Religious authority, Blackamerican Muslims have experienced great difficulty in addressing American reality on the basis of the super-tradition of Islam.   Like Black Christians before them, Blackamerican Muslims will have to pass through an evolution to finding ways to reconcile blackness, Americanness and Islam. They will have to execute this in a manner that neither reduces their religion to a cultural performance nor converts it into just another secular ideology in religious garb.

Without question, he says, this is the challenge facing Blackamerican Muslims in the Third Resurrection. It should be noted that this is not a unique challenge. Marshall Hodgson noted that within the dialogue launched by the advent of Islam, almost from the start there came to be conflicting sets of presuppositions about what Islam should involve[58].

Accordingly, I believe that any relevant expression of Al-Islam must not only connect on a spiritual/ religious level, the sociopolitical, cultural and economic issues of the community must also be addressed. The fact is that every authentic expression of Al-Islam, including the revival[59] of Al-Islam through the revelation of the Qur'an and Prophetic career of the Prophet Muhammad (PBUH) has connected all aspects of living and culture in a meaningful way.

The Arabic word Deen[60], often translated "religion", as used in the Holy Qur'an should be properly understood as a complete life system, not just a set of religious rituals. Real religion, Deen, spiritually and religiously connects the means of life with a belief in The Mercifully Compassionate and Just Creator. Deen that is next to Allah inspires a group of people to establish a compassionately just, life sustaining system in a way that nurtures the common good.[61]

The revival of Al-Islam in 7th century Arabia, confirmed the true and exclusive object of faith while simultaneously addressing issues related to a widening gap between rich and poor and equitable justice under the law for all citizens regardless of gender or class. The information that comes to us in the authentic Sunnah and Seerah[62] of the Prophet (PBUH) is reflective of a 7th century Arabian version of a just society due to the impact of the revelation of the Holy Qur'an. The Qur'an was revealed by Allah to be the primary standard by which a Muslim evaluates situations.

Allah instructs Muslims to, "Strive with it, a great striving!" [63] The Prophet Muhammad (PBUH) is reported to have stated in his farewell sermon, "And I have left among you a thing which if you adhered to, you will never be misguided after me, the Book of Allah"[64][65]. Allah refers to the Qur'an by many names in the Qur'an such as The Guidance[66], The Light[67], The Wisdom[68] and The Criterion [69]. It is intended as guidance for the entire creation.[70] It is an article of Islamic faith that there is a revolutionary effect caused by the positive response by a people to Allah's revelation.

> **47:2**. And those who believe and do righteous deeds and believe in what has been sent down upon Muhammad and it is the truth from their Lord – He will remove from them their misdeeds and amend their condition.

Using the Qur'an as the primary guidance, my firm belief is that if that next step in the Black American Muslim story is not a step made with individual and collective self confidence and certainty with an understanding of Al-Islam that synthesizes the Black American Experience and culture with the higher purposes of Al-Islam as expressed in Allah's revelation, all the other analysis that is being undertaken by some or our brightest scholars and Imams will be moot. Accordingly, my personal belief is that the tradition of Al-Islam is an essential reference point for analysis and not imitation for Black American, or any other contemporary Muslims.[71]

There needs to continue to be a focused effort to peel the theological and cultural onion often purported to be Al-Islam as an essential activity for reform and for the continued development of the Black American and American Muslim community. The term commonly used in the Black American Muslim community to describe those versions Al-Islam hopelessly entangled with another culture is *His*lam.

In some ways, signs of this next wave of Black American Muslims is evident by the more common presence of Muslims in all aspects of public life, a trend that may be spectacular in its ordinariness and lack of fanfare.

A distinguishing feature of those that help to promote a culturally calibrated and refined understanding of Al-islam may be the internal disposition and insight of those individuals that are expressed on contemporary issues inspired by the Qur'an and authentic Sunnah of Prophet Muhammad (PBUH), not in outer appearance. To the point, Allah instructed Prophets Musa (PBUH) and Harun (PBUH) to speak to Pharaoh "with gentle speech that perhaps he may be reminded or fear [Allah]"[72]. One of the great Sufis[73], when describing a Gnostic stated that when the Gnostic is with the people of any place, he finds in it the same things that they find. While he is there he articulates that place's qualities so that its people may profit.[74]

Without a healthy sense of self, Black American Muslims, may be susceptible to measuring our understanding of the Al-Islam, not by an understanding of the Qur'an and Sunnah as informed by our experience but rather to judge our understanding of Al-Islam by the contemporary and past experience of others. Accordingly, we would unwittingly position ourselves as people that deny the signs of our unique experience, thereby forming a shell of a people easily manipulated away from causes that naturally evolve from our experience. Allah has revealed:

> **7:181** And among those We created is a community which guides by truth and thereby establishes justice.
> **7:182** But those who deny Our signs – We will progressively lead them [to destruction] from where they do not know.

We would instead be acting in accordance with the disposition described by the infamous statement by Carter G. Woodson:

> If you can control a man's thinking, you don't have to worry about his actions. You do not have to tell him not to stand here or go yonder. He will find his "proper place" and will stay in it. You do not need to send him to the back door, he will go without being told. In fact, if there is no back door, he will cut one for his special benefit. His education makes it necessary.[75]

The fact is that the Qur'an and Sunnah envision a continuous process of revival through the contribution of new peoples adding their unique cultural perspective to the on-going dialogue of Al-Islam[76]. This has been characteristic of Muslim communities from the beginning of Al-Islam. It should not be forgotten that according to Islamic theology, Monotheism was established by Prophets Ibrahim (PBUH) and Ishmael (PBUH) in Arabia. The pure monotheism gradually gave way to a polytheistic worship and was revived as a result of the Prophet Muhammad's (PBUH) prophetic mission.

I find that students and admirers of Islamic societies sometimes overlook the length of time and process between the initial engagement Al-Islam and its broad acceptance by a community. For instance, the Islamic movement led Sheik Uthman Dan Fodio in northern Nigeria culminated in the late eighteen to the nineteenth century. Although Islam was established by 1500, it was certainly not generally accepted.

What seems to have happened is that individual Muslims from the peripheral areas of North Africa and Egypt — traders seeking the gold and slaves of the Sudan, and scholars after the lucrative patronage of the courts—came into the Habe kingdoms and settled. They formed the nuclei of small Islamic communities that gradually began to affect the surrounding animist culture of the native people.

The first stage was the nominal acceptance of Islam by some of the chiefs and courtiers. But this amounted to little more than the adoption of Islamic names in addition to indigenous titles, and participation in certain Islamic rites—for instance, the annual sacrifices—and perhaps attendance at Friday mosque. This much identification with Islam was regarded as prestigious by the chiefs' still-pagan subjects.

But they were certainly not prepared to see their traditional cults wholly abandoned; and the chiefs were probably unable to accept Islam wholeheartedly, even had they wished to do so. The result was that the two cultures existed side by side, and sometimes merged to produce "mixed" Islam—some Islamic practices carried on with animist customs and rites.[77]

I believe there is always a period of "mixed" Islam, from its introduction to a community to its universal acceptance where there is effectively a cultural shake out so that an appropriate implementation of Al-Islam is naturally embraced by the mass of that culture. The specific example of the Sokoto community is not unique. African Traditional Religions (ATR), in those areas of the Western Sudan where the Muslims carved out a foothold from which they have not been dislodged to this day, rarely experienced at the hands of Islam the bitter antagonism they experienced from Protestant Christianity when the evangelical missionary societies arrived near the end of the eighteenth century.

Islam sometimes blended imperceptibly with ATR, content to permit Africans to call themselves Muslims without demanding more than minimal changes in belief structure and lifestyle. Much of West African culture, in terms of totem, rites of purification and invocation, reverence of the ancestors, and the use of amulets and talismans, was left undisturbed as long as the pillars of Islam were upheld and Allah was entreated to make a person "a better Muslim."

It may be said that in consequence ATR was enriched by the Arabic language, the Arabic emphasis on education and the universal brotherhood of a highly diverse humanity, rather than rudely stamped out by stern and often racist expatriates bent upon condemning everything African and saving the souls of the heathen[78]. It is because of this reconciliation period on the path of Islamization that I believe blindly imitating precedents of other communituties is inconsistent with the spirit of the revelation of the Qur'an and Sunnah of the Prophet (PBUH)[79] and the pattern of development of Al-Islam in other societies.

I would like to note that the community of Imam Warith Deen Muhammad[80] has always advocated an understanding of Al-Islam that evolves out of cultural experience. [81] According to Imam Muhammad, Blacks, should find an Islam whose meaning would be determined within the Black community and whose focus would be on the betterment of Black life.[82] Imam Faheem Shuaibe states that, "the message and mission of Imam Muhammed should be understood as the restoration of the So-called American Negro as new entrant to mainstream Al-Islam after their emancipation from the Nation of Islam to a correct and effective perception and application of Al-Islam in America.

A Quranic-based perception that is, by and large, independent of any other spirit Immigrant Muslim or Non-Muslim.   His mission is to show them how to serve Allah uniquely and autonomously from the core of their natural being's history, circumstances and destiny.[83]   At the same time, Imam Muhammad consistently taught we are all a part of the human family and stated, "this religion doesn't come to teach us about the Black family or the White family. This religion came to teach us about the human family. So the excellence of man is the excellence of all men, the excellence of a human being is the excellence of all human beings".[84]

To the point, It goes without saying that responding to issues in the Black community necessarily involves addressing issues in the society as a whole given the fact that the Black community and larger society are inextricably linked. I believe that we need to continue to build on the confidence resulting from past and current efforts to interpret the Qur'an and Sunnah in a manner that is relevant and appropriate for our experience. We should be ready to offer our unique perspective on Al-Islam and to help revive the understanding of Al-Islam within appropriate contexts[85].

We also need to be secure enough in our relationship with Allah that we are not shaken if our perspective is not solicited and the face of an "authentic" Muslim in the media is portrayed as anything except indigenous or Black.[86] Further, Black American Muslims will be better positioned to dialogue with people of all ethnicities from a position of neither awe nor resentment but from a healthy position of mutual respect. It is already common to see young people of all ethnicities intermingling and socializing on college campuses.[87]

At the end of the day, if Black American Muslims can draw a straight line between the guidance the Qur'an and Sunnah to stable marriages, well adjusted children and vibrant communities there will be lines of people asking for our perspective on Al-Islam. The Prophet of Allah is reported to have said:

> "Not to wish to be the like of except two men: A man whom Allah has taught the Qur'an and he recites it during the hours of the night and during the hours of the day, and his neighbor listens to him and says, 'I wish I had been given what has been given to so-and-so, so that I might do what he does'; and a man whom Allah has given wealth and he spends it on what is just and right, whereupon another man may say, 'I wish I had been given what so-and-so has been given, for then I would do what he does.' "[88]

Allah's Attributes and the Framework for Authenticity

That Allah wants us to own our experience and have certainty in its authenticity is clear in the Qur'an and Sunnah. Divine Decree is an article of faith in Al-Islam. The specific time, place and circumstance, the complete context both internal and external, of our lives and its context is not an accident. Everything is created with the measure[89] of Allah.

> **13:8** Allah knows what every female carries and what the wombs lose [prematurely] or exceed and everything with Him is by due measure
> **13:9** [He is] Knower of the unseen and the witnessed, the Grand, the Exalted.

At the same time everything is by the will of Allah, we have a degree of choice within the broad parameter of Allah's will. The ability to exercise judgment is one of the qualities that distinguish human beings. The Prophet Muhammad (PBUH) has advised wisely that the details of this dynamic are beyond our human comprehension to completely understand so we should not spend excessive amounts of time in philosophical discussions and disputes about the concept.[90]

Taking the Prophet's (PBUH) advice, I don't obsess on this subject, but I believe I have developed a working understanding of Divine Decree that has helped me to reconcile the seemingly contradictory theological concepts of Allah's infinite power and our free will. My approach toward a working understanding of this dynamic is to imagine that each of us arrives at a spiritual intersection numerous times a day by the will of Allah. We have the opportunity with every action, interaction and within the context of every relationship to choose a response that is consistent with higher values of Al-Islam (Submission to the Will of Allah) expressed in Allah's names, or to respond in a way that is inconsistent with the higher values and purposes of Al-Islam.

This is a spiritual intersection I call the intersection of Destiny and Opportunity. We are provided the opportunity to turn to Allah and to achieve a spiritual nearness to Allah by our faith and good intentions if followed up with sincere good actions[91].

As advised by the Prophet Muhammad (PBUH), good deeds are the manifestation of sincere good intentions[92]. Our good deeds should be for Allah alone. One of the names of Allah's attributes is At-Tawwab, The Accepter of Repentance. So turning towards Allah with certainty of belief through sincere good intentions and actions is a practical way of Dhikring (remembering) Allah.

The Arabic root word for this attribute of Allah means; To repent towards God; to turn one's-self in a repentant manner; to relent towards men. [93] The choice to turn towards Allah starts internally by accepting yourself and moving along the spiritual paths of Allah through good deeds[94] from a Muslim to a Believer.[95]

In all of this, it is important to not lose sight of the fact that human beings are not perfect. We all make mistakes. Living authentically means that we accept that we often fall short and that we don't always choose the higher, nobler course. What is important is that we take responsibility for our mistakes, turn to Allah in repentance and continue to live life. The only sin Allah does not accept is the sin of associating partners with Allah.

> **4:48**. Indeed, Allah does not forgive association with Him, but He forgives what is less than that for whom He wills. And he who associates others with Allah has certainly fabricated a tremendous sin.
> **4:49**. Have you not seen those who claim themselves to be pure? Rather, Allah purifies whom He wills, and injustice is not done to them, [even] as much as a thread [inside a date seed].

I submit that our personal framework for authenticity starts with an understanding of the Names of Allah and their meaning. The total understanding includes their theological, scientific and sociological implications. Allah has revealed in the Holy Qur'an:

> **7:180**. And to Allah belong the best names, so invoke Him by them. And leave [the company of] those who practice deviation concerning His names. They will be recompensed for what they have been doing.

> **59:24**. He is Allah, the Creator, the Inventor, the Fashioner; to Him belong the best names. Whatever is in the heavens and earth is exalting Him. And He is the Exalted in Might, the Wise.

In Allah's creative names, it is easy to see the Allah has the ability to create, invent, form and fashion as he wills. The Qur'an is clear that our creation and lives are intentional and with purpose. The following ayah from the Qur'an highlight the purposeful framework for our experience. Further, with regard to Black culture, the ayah support the idea that the various levels of culture, subculture and their corresponding sociology are the product of Allah's Divine will.

Our creation is as a single soul:

> **31: 28** Your creation and your resurrection will not be but as that of a single soul. Indeed, Allah is Hearing and Seeing.

Even before our soul was placed in a particular body, our natures were embedded with the knowledge of correct belief:

> **7:172** And [mention] when your Lord took from the children of Adam – from their loins – their descendants and made them testify of themselves, [saying to them], "Am I not your Lord?"

35

They said, "Yes, we have testified." [This] – lest you should say on the Day of Resurrection, "Indeed, we were of this unaware."
7:173 Or [lest] you say, "It was only that our fathers associated [others in worship] with Allah before, and we were but descendants after them. Then would You destroy us for what the falsifiers have done?"
7:174 And thus do We [explain in] detail the verses, and perhaps they will return.[96]

Allah created and formed everything:

86: 1 Exalt the name of your Lord, the Most High,
86:2 Who created and proportioned

Everything Allah created is perfect:

32:7 Who perfected everything which He created and began the creation of man from clay.

Allah governs the reproductive process and makes our bodies:

23: 12. And certainly did We create man from an extract of clay.
23:13 Then We placed him as a sperm-drop in a firm lodging [i.e., the womb].
23:14 Then We made the sperm-drop into a clinging clot, and We made the clot into a lump [of flesh], and We made [from] the lump, bones, and We covered the bones with flesh; then We developed him into another creation. So blessed is Allah, the best of creators.
23:15. Then indeed, after that you are to die.
23:16. Then indeed you, on the Day of Resurrection, will be resurrected.

Allah breathes his spirit into us:

> **32:9** Then He proportioned him and breathed into him from His [created] soul and made for you hearing and vision and hearts [i.e., intellect]; little are you grateful.

We are born in a physiological context. We inherit DNA and other traits from parents and other ancestors

> **32:8** Then He made his posterity out of the extract of a liquid disdained.

Human beings, like many species of the animal and insect worlds operate within a social context.

> **6:38** And there is no creature on [or within] the earth or bird that flies with its wings except [that they are] communities like you. We have not neglected in the Register a thing. Then unto their Lord they will be gathered.

Your family and social relationships are critical to your identity. Even at the judgment you are not separated from your people.
:

> **84:6** O mankind, indeed you are laboring toward your Lord with [great] exertion and will meet it.
> **84:7** Then as for he who is given his record in his right hand,
> **84:8** He will be judged with an easy account
> **84:9** And return to his people in happiness.

A central premise of the Dhikr of Authenticity is that our authenticity and inner peace associated with it is a condition that is inherent in our being in the here and now. It is something to be reaffirmed internally with Allah, not something that must be proven to others.

It is ours for reclaiming, it is by our own actions and due to our self doubt that it has been lost. Allah has revealed:

> **13:9** [He is] Knower of the unseen and the witnessed, the Grand, the Exalted.
> **13:11** … Verily, Allah will not change the (good) condition of a people as long as they do not change their state (of goodness) themselves.[97]
>
> **59:19** And be not like those who forgot Allah, so He made them forget themselves. Those are the defiantly disobedient.

The Black Experience

The Black experience informs the sociology of Black people. That sociology has been shaped by the encounter and struggle with White Supremacy. It is impossible to overstate the real and imagined impact of the doctrine and implementation of White Supremacy on the psyche of Black people. Dr. Cornel West observed that any serious examination of black culture should begin what W.E.B. DuBois dubbed, in Faustian terms, the "spiritual strivings" of black people — the dogged determination to survive and subsist, the tenacious will to persevere, persist and maybe even prevail. These "strivings" occur within the whirlwind of white supremacy — that is, as responses to the vicious attacks on black beauty, black intelligence, black moral character, black capability, and black possibility.

To put it bluntly, every major institution in American society – churches, universities, courts, academies of science, governments, economics, newspapers, magazines, television, film, and others – attempted to exclude black people from the human family in the names of white supremacist ideology. This unrelenting assault on black humanity produced the fundamental condition of black culture – that of black invisibility and namelessness.[98]

For me, the venture of Black Strivings can be summed up by one Arabic word, Jihad. The concept of Jihad in the religion of Al-Islam is a comprehensive word whose root meaning is "to be diligent" and "a striving with might and main".[99].   The struggle for justice in Al-Islam is a relentless effort using every means at your disposal provided that the struggle is conducted within the bounds prescribed in the Qur'an and authentic Sunnah of the Prophet Muhammad (PBUH)[100]. According to the Dictionary of the Qur'an, the word Jihad is defined as, "Exerting of one's utmost power in the contending with an object of disapprobation"[101].

It is a single term that captures the spirit of Frederick Douglas' famous saying, "This struggle may be a moral one, or it may be a physical one, and it may be both moral and physical, but it must be a struggle. Power concedes nothing without a demand". [102]

While the group effort to confront all forms injustice including racism are valid Islamic impulses, the Prophet (PBUH) has advised against extreme forms of nationalism clarifying that it is not prohibited to love your people; it is prohibited to assist your people in wrong doing. [103] Allah often times checks one people by way of another in order to demonstrate the universal principle of justice within a particular context[104]. However, over reacting to injustice by developing methodologies and doctrines that are inconsistent with the higher values of Al-Islam that, when measured against the standard of the Qur'an and Sunnah of the Prophet Muhammad (PBUH) is prohibited.

Declaration of Faith

The shahada, testifying that Allah is the sole object of worship, the Prophet Muhammad (PBUH) is the final messenger and that you will not negate that affirmation with inconsistent actions or beliefs is the foundation of the personal tauheed of Al-Islam as revealed in the Qur'an. The shahada has external and internal implications.

Externally it means there is no object of worship except Allah. As Allah is the sole creator, all creation works harmoniously and is consistent with itself[105]. During the days of the Prophet Muhammad (PBUH), people literally worshipped idolatrous representations of 'gods". Today we might worship our status, position, lifestyle or wealth. Some societies imagined their race, culture or civilization as inherently superior to another, sometimes reinforced by a privileged or exclusive position with a deity.

I was raised in a Christian family, but among the tenants[106] of Christian theology that I could never reconcile is that the biblical Black Hebrews, and those that adopted Judaism after them, have an exclusive relationship with Allah that others have to somehow appropriate to earn Allah's grace. [107] Islamic monotheism holds that there is balance and equity inherent in the creation since everything comes from The One Creator. Accordingly there is no inherent superiority or inferiority for any people. Allah has revealed:

> **23:91** Allah has not taken any son, nor has there ever been with Him any deity. [If there had been], then each deity would have taken what it created, and some of them would have sought to overcome others. Exalted is Allah above what they describe [concerning Him].

The internal implication of taking shahada and embracing Tauheed as a personally organizing principle necessarily starts with the development and maintenance of a healthy self-respect. Allah's Apostle (peace be upon him) said, "A believer is self-respecting and Allah is extremely self respecting".[108]

Some people, in their heart of hearts do not really believe that they are worthy, deserving, have value or are a unique sign of Allah. This self doubt may come from accepting certain negative stereo types or images, family histories that include psychological or physical abuse, chemical dependency or systematic lack of achievement. Some may have "friends" that really don't want anything for themselves or you and who constantly hold you back.

To take shahada and to embrace Tauheed as a personally organizing principle means that a person begins to disassociate from all negative influences and thoughts on the path to developing a healthy self respect. This self respect is due to the recognition of the fact that each one of us is a part of Allah's creation and counted among the diversity of his signs. Allah has revealed:

> 30:20 And of His signs is that He created you from dust; then, suddenly you were human beings dispersing [throughout the earth].

> 30:22 And of His signs is the creation of the heavens and the earth and the diversity of your languages and your colors. Indeed in that are signs for those of knowledge.

The Prophet Muhammad (PBUH) is reported to have said in his farewell sermon:

> All mankind is from Adam and Eve, an Arab has no superiority over a non-Arab nor a non-Arab has any superiority over an Arab; also a white has no superiority over black nor a black has any superiority over white except by piety and good action.[109]

As we are all a part of Allah's creation there is no inherent superiority from one group, culture, experience or history over another as each of these is due to the Qadr[110] of Allah. As diversity is one of the signs of Allah, an indicator of the presence of Al-Islam is the reinforcement, not the obliteration of a culture. The ultimately distinguishing characteristic of a culture is its Allah consciousness. We are instructed by Allah to learn from one another.

> **49:13** O mankind, indeed We have created you from male and female and made you peoples and tribes that you may know one another. Indeed, the most noble of you in the sight of Allah is the most righteous of you. Indeed, Allah is Knowing and Acquainted.

To believe in Allah is to accept the concept of Tauheed; Oneness. The Oneness of Allah, Humanity and Creation. The struggle is to really believe and practice what is professed, internally and externally. It starts with accepting, embracing, loving yourself and all that you are. That is easier said than done when the Black experience includes a constant battle to strive against all the overt and covert messages designed in the structure of the society that to be Black is to inherently be the opposite of smart, beautiful, nice, good...

To be Black can often times mean finding oneself in the position of not receiving the presumption of the benefit of the doubt. This is a subtle, often overlooked component of White Privilege[111].

That knowledge and belief in yourself must be embraced as a starting point for advancement was emphasized by W.E.B. Dubois. DuBois said as a consequence of acquiring self knowledge through study and referring to Black people as a group, "He began to have a dim feeling that, to attain his place in the world, *he must be himself, and not another"*[112]. [emphasis mine]

DuBois' belief in the power of education resonates with the Qur'an and Sunnah as the very first revelation of the Qur'an to the Prophet Muhammad (PBUH) was to "Read!"[113] Harriet Tubman is reported to have said, "If I could have convinced more slaves that they were slaves, I could have freed thousands more"[114]. Allah has revealed a parable to describe those that ignore knowledge and deny the signs of Allah:

> **7:175**. And recite to them, [O Muhammad], the news of him to whom We gave [knowledge of] Our signs, but he detached himself from them; so Satan pursued him, and he became of the deviators.
> **7:176**. And if We had willed, We could have elevated him thereby, but he adhered [instead] to the earth and followed his own desire. So his example is like that of the dog: if you chase him, he pants, or if you leave him, he [still] pants. That is the example of the people who denied Our signs. So relate the stories that perhaps they will give thought.

It is clear to me that that only the self respecting soul can have a hope of achieving a level of felicity, by the Will of Allah. Self respect is one of the manifestations of the Shahada.

The Next Wave

I believe that in the continued conversation on the next step of Black American Muslim development, there will emerge a Next Wave of Black American Muslims that with love, faith, humility and certainty will affirm that they stand at an intersection of destiny and opportunity as they will influence the conversation around the development of Al-Islam first in the Black American community and then in the larger Muslim community.

I believe that this conversation will occur in large part out of the sight of the media spotlight and in networks of families and close friends. DuBois argued that the development of all people evolves from four sources: the precepts of parents, the sight of peers, the opinion of the majority, and the traditions of the past. [115] [116] Every family goes through successive waves of evolution as one generation gives way to another through the natural cycles of life. This week's funeral will give way to next week's marriage or baby shower.

Coming out of the intimate network of family, near neighbors and friends, I believe that among the characteristics of the next wave of Muslims in the Black American community will be their ability to reconcile to their satisfaction their belief in the fundamental principles of Al-Islam expressed primarily in the Holy Qur'an and authentic hadith[117] sources while sustaining relationships with Muslim and non-Muslim friends, family and colleagues, all the while embracing their citizenship and culture as they are completely integrated into society. Accordingly, they will not be overly concerned with the perception or approval of others as the unique history of Black American Islam continues to unfold.

Transcending the peculiar sensation DuBois called double-consciousness, this sense of always looking at one's self through the eyes of others[118], will provide for the development of coalitions of independently oriented Muslims to establish masajid and to organize to support and advocate for worthy, and particularly local causes.

Some of the qualities of this next wave may include:

1. Driven primarily by the belief in One Unique God, Allah and Tauheed on a personal level[119];

2. Embrace the primacy of the Holy Qur'an as the ultimate authority for divine guidance[120];

3. Have a love for the Prophet Muhammad (PBUH) as a kind of "Spiritual Mentor" and seek the best, contextual understanding of the Prophet's life from authentic sources that are consistent with the Qur'an[121];

4. Are scrupulous with their acceptance of hadith[122];

5. Tend to be internally driven and more "Spiritual" than "Religious". This enables an ability to see a bigger picture and to distinguish (though not abandon) rituals and the values and results the rituals are intended to produce;

6. Embrace the spiritual equality of Woman as an obvious matter of fact[123];

7. Due to spiritual inclination, likely attracted to the opportunity to explore spirituality through Sufism. However, they sidestep the temptation to engage in an alternate set of "spiritual rituals" and will engage in what I call a "Practical Tassawuf[124]" that focuses on your unseen self, your psyche and ego and explores family of origin[125] issues to determine root causes that get in

the way of exhibiting the values of patience, justice, forgiveness, mercy etc… expressed in the Qur'an, Allah's names and attributes and Sunnah of Prophet Muhammad (PBUH)[126].

8. Understand that there has been and always will be a diversity of opinion in the Ummah and are therefore able to exercise a "Fiqh of Unity", the fundamental principle being that there is a range of valid expressions of the faith and that a difference of opinion does not make one a Kafir (unbeliever). I personally believe that many of us are on the straight path albeit in different lanes.[127]

9. Family focused and active in their families and communities[128];

10. Are not driven primarily by Anger in a conscious or unconscious way[129];

11. Confident in the authenticity of their personal, family and cultural experiences within the context of the larger society and the unique expression of Al-Islam that is inevitably produced. Therefore, they don't need to be validated by others;

12. Are objective and not romantic in their historical and contemporary assessment of the Ummah;[130]

13. Don't go by the labels, Sunni, Shia or Sufi per se. Allah does not use those terms in the Holy Qur'an[131][132];

14. Form partnerships with individuals of all traditions around common causes that are mutually beneficial and are beneficial to society[133]

15. Are wary of individuals and "scholars" that are trained in a narrow application of Al-Islam to the exclusion of other legitimate expressions of the Deen[134].

Dawud Abdur-Rahman

A Way Forward – The Alignment of Causes

There is a clear imperative in the Holy Qur'an to believe and to work righteously.[135] [136] A spiritual, inside/ out, perspective based on the higher values intents and purposes of Al-Islam that engages the range of people in your sphere of influence based primarily on your relationship with Allah will result in an authentic expression of Al-Islam that is relevant.

This type of an approach will result in an alignment of causes, something that Malcolm X always understood and had to address as he evolved from the theology of the Nation of Islam to an understanding of Al-Islam consistent with the Holy Qur'an. He was so effective at aligning causes that even though he repudiated Christianity, some Christians were willing to say in those days, "The God that spoke by the prophets and in the fullness of time by his Son, now speaks to us through Brother Malcolm."[137]

Malcolm was one our most brilliant and eloquent spokesman for Black Religion – the "spiritual strivings: (DuBois) – of oppressed and scattered Africans who refused to surrender their humanity under enslavement and never lost sight of the freedom and justice they believed were God-given.[138] I believe that is the reason it is not uncommon even today to see Malcolm's picture displayed in Black American churches.

Allah has revealed:

> **4:36**. Worship Allah and associate nothing with Him, and to parents do good, and to relatives, orphans, the needy, the near neighbor, the neighbor farther away, the companion at your side, the traveler, and those whom your right hands possess. Indeed, Allah does not like those who are self-deluding and boastful,
> **4:37**. Who are stingy and enjoin upon [other] people stinginess and conceal what Allah has given them of His bounty – and We have prepared for the disbelievers a humiliating punishment –

4:38. And [also] those who spend of their wealth to be seen by the people and believe not in Allah nor in the Last Day. And he to whom Satan is a companion – then evil is he as a companion.

Declaring that there is no object of worship except Allah should be a supremely self empowering act. Allah does not require us to be perfect, only to strive diligently to make our intentions pure and aligned with divine guidance. With Tauheed as an organizing principle we can begin to align our thoughts, psyche and actions from the inside out and to try to be a catalyst in bringing peace, safety and security in our individual spheres of influence. Notwithstanding every Muslim's spiritual and psychological citizenship in the worldwide Muslim Ummah, one need not look exclusively to another part of the world to align your relationship with Allah while   ignoring worthy causes adjacent to you.

There is need of good Fathers, Mothers, Siblings, "God" Parents, Neighbors and family members in your immediate circle. Personally, I feel a great sense of debt to my Brother in law. He is not a Muslim, but he effectively dropped the "in law" part of his title and was in every sense a big brother to me as I was growing up. Taking me under his wing and teaching me what I call day to "Day to Day Deen". The things that boys need to learn from men, how to dress, save my money, fight, tie a tie, about woman. Somewhere in the distance of Black history I can hear the echo of Booker T. Washington urging us to, "Cast down your bucket where you are![139]."

There is an on-going conversation about the relevance of Al-Islam in the Black American community. I find that many of the good examples of the relevance of Muslims, especially in the Black community, for instance, in Bill Cosby's "call outs" and books, are references to the Nation of Islam; not references to Muslims in the "orthodox" communities.

Authors Bill Cosby and Alvin Poussaint observed, "Although they have made their own share of mistakes like everyone else the Black Muslims have never been the kind of folks to sit in the back of anyone's bus. What is more, they have always believed in their community. Neither of your authors is a member of the Nation of Islam, but we know what we see".[140]

The "Islam" of the Nation of Islam is a manifestation of Black Religion, a principle component being a pragmatic, folk-oriented, holy protest against anti-black racism[141]. Unfortunately, as some movements migrated towards expressions of Islam that are more consistent with the Qur'an and Sunnah of the Prophet Muhammad (PBUH) the migration they also sometimes broke from Black Religion.

Sherman Jackson discusses this dynamic in <u>Islam and the Black American, Looking Toward the Third Resurrection</u>. He states, "In all of this, however, perhaps the most lamentable development was the seemingly reversed effect Islam was exerting on the pathologies and dysfunctionalities of the urban ghetto. Beyond the explicitly religious vices, for example, illicit sex or alcohol, consumption, Islam was fast losing its significance as a fortifier of indigenous constructions of such values as manly pride, fiscal responsibility, or civic consciousness.

Whereas under the "Islam" of the Honorable Elijah Muhammad, education, work, and community-uplift were synonymous with Black Muslim, Sunni Islam was increasingly being invoked as a reason not to work (for the infidel), not to be educated (in the infidel's institutions), and not to be involved in the (infidel) community. At least as far as the Old Guard was concerned, one could now almost assume that the stricter a Blackamerican Muslim adhered to Islam, the less educated, less gainfully employed and the less civic minded he or she was likely to be.

In short, on the new, immigrant-influenced understanding of Islam, Sunnism was in many ways becoming a cause rather than a solution to the problem of Blackamerican Muslim dysfunctionality in America." [142] I see this inverse relationship between Islamic orthodoxy and relevancy as ironic because as Sulyman Nyang states, "As history would have it, the efforts of the late Elijah Muhammad have done more for the multiplication of Muslim members than any missionary work from other groups of Muslims in the country". [143]

The challenge of addressing cultural relevance while adhering to the Qur'an and Sunnah of the Prophet is critical to devising a healthy path forward. I have to admit that my initial image of a culturally relevant Islam is based in large part by my interactions growing up in West Philadelphia and interacting with friends that were in the Nation of Islam. I saw former gang members become helpers as opposed to predators in the community after joining the Nation. I unfortunately also saw Brothers and Sisters who accepted "orthodox" Islam, completely change their manner of dress, names, diction and socializing as they withdrew from the community and sometimes family. It is encouraging to see more and more Muslims understand that synthesizing the Qur'an, Sunnah and Black Religion and Black Strivings is essential to produce valid expressions of Al-Islam in the Black community.

Accordingly, I believe the path forward for relevance is similar to Malcolm X's. He continually evolved, but never lost sight of the root of the tree from which he sprang or its causes [144]. Esoteric or rigid interpretations of the Qur'an and Sunnah under the guise of gaining greater spiritual insight or religious orthodoxy will not engender an Al-Islam that has meaning and relevance. Sojourner Truth said, "Religion without humanity is very poor human stuff" [145]

The answer lies in human kindness and connectedness, remembering Allah by his attribute, Ar-Rahman an attribute of Allah that means "merciful and compassionate" and whose root meaning is "to be merciful, have mercy upon"[146]. Seyyed Hossein Nasr explains:

> "The term *rahmah* which means both "mercy" and "compassion" is related to the two Divine Names of *al-Rahman*, the Infinitely Good, and *al-Rahim*, the All-Merciful, with which every chapter of the Qur'an except one commences. They are also the Names with which every daily human acts are consecrated. Because these names are interwoven into every aspect of the Muslims, life is thereby wrapped in Divine Goodness, Mercy and Compassion, which are inextricably associated with the Arabic word *al-rahman*. Moreover, this word is related to the Arabic term for 'womb", *rahim* Therefore, it might be said that the word issues from the womb of Divine Mercy and Compassion. "[147]

I understand all of this to mean that a focus on human kindness, relationships and in practically offering solutions that address issues for instance with the so called "Black Agenda". Issues such as family, jobs, retirement income, education, cost of living, crime etc[148] ... is paramount for the Servants of Allah, Most Merciful. These issues may be more acute in some Black communities, however, they are issues that are important to all communities. Allah has revealed:

> **22:41**. [And they are] those who, if We give them authority in the land, establish prayer and give zakah and enjoin what is right and forbid what is wrong. And to Allah belongs the outcome of [all] matters.

The Prophet Muhammad (PBUH) has offered an outline to organize any experience and culture within an Islamic framework. The five pillars of Al-Islam are accepted by a vast majority of Muslims.

53

A Bedouin came to the Prophet and said, "Tell me of such a deed as will make me enter Paradise, if I do it." The Prophet (p.b.u.h) said, "Worship Allah, and worship none along with Him, offer the (five) prescribed compulsory prayers perfectly, pay the compulsory Zakat, and fast the month of Ramadan." The Bedouin said, "By Him, in Whose Hands my life is, I will not do more than this." When he (the Bedouin) left, the Prophet said, "Whoever likes to see a man of Paradise, then he may look at this man." [149]

I believe the wisdom of the report from our beloved Prophet (PBUH) is to help us to prioritize and to identify areas that should be the focus and anchor for moving forward in the continued process of Islamization. He prophesized that there would come a time when he who observes one-tenth of what was then prescribed will be saved[150]. Certainly an Islam that embraces Black culture and that incorporates the five pillars of Al-Islam, may not look like an authentic expression if someone's baseline for authenticity is rooted another culture and/ or time.

W.E.B. DuBois stated that Black people did not engage the struggle for justice in America empty handed, we came with a culturally base expressed initially in through Spirituality and Music.[151] He asserted that we are that people whose subtle sense of song has given America its only American music, its only American fairy tales, its only touch of pathos and humor amid its mad money-getting plutocracy[152].

I understand DuBois' assertions about music both as a specific contribution and also as representative of and included in the broader understanding of culture. To the point, DuBois described the temporal objective of "spiritual strivings: "to be a co-worker in the kingdom of culture, to escape both death and isolation, and to husband and use his best powers[153]."

W.E.B. DuBois rebelled against religious teaching that focused on empty rituals and that undermined Black culture. Clearly we bring much more to the table now and we should not lose what we have, as we respect the cultures of others and as we continue to evolve as Muslims.

I find that Black American Muslims that do not forget the root from which they sprung, take a position similar that offered by reformist minded Muslims such as Tariq Ramadan[154] who says that Muslims in the West share an identity informed by multiple subcultures[155]. The Qur'an and Sunnah do not prescribe a blind acceptance of rituals and customs devoid of meaning or that obliterate the culture of a people as a necessarily valid implementation of Al-Islam.

One scholarly opinion predicts that culture fills whatever discretionary space eludes the principles of sharia virtually assuring that popular culture and contemporary Islam will continue to dispute personal and social matters[156]. I would go further. I believe the ongoing dialogue regarding the development of Al-Islam should also include the degree to which culture informed the classical understanding of sharia in the first place as a part of the acknowledgement that culture was created and exists by the will of Allah. Further, that culture is specific and not universal.

Most sociologists of religion will agree that religion does much the same thing for all sorts and conditions of peoples. But it is a matter of serious debate whether a specific religion of a specific people can be transmitted in toto to another people – even in the same geographical location – without certain substantive changes due to ethnicity, custom, social structure, and many other factors. [157]

The Islamic discourse is centered primarily on the synthesis of the Qur'an and Sunnah with the cultural norms of a people. Qur'anic Arabic, its vocabulary. Idiom, style, and syntax is the language of pre-Islamic and Prophetic milieu was well known and understood by the Arabs of that period.

The Qur'an's primary discourse is directed at the Qurayshites of Makkah and it is for that reason it has been reported in hadith that it was revealed in the dialects of the Qurayshites. This language represents Arab culture and society at the dawn of Islam, a culture and society far much different from contemporary Arabic because our language keep on evolving due to social changes[158]. Accordingly, the calibration of understanding of the Qur'an to the contemporary conditions is the responsibility of every Muslim people.

One of the most critical areas where the implementation of Al-Islam in a contemporary context is playing out revolves around woman. Malcolm X famously said "No nation can rise higher than its woman". With regard to chronology, it has always been pointed out that the Qur'an brought many changes to the status of woman and for their consideration in society.[159]

Umar Ibn al-Kattab was quoted as saying: 'By God, we did not used to pay attention to woman in the Jahiliyyah until God said about them in the Qur'an what is said, and gave them their share in matters.' Still, the continued change which the Qur'an put into motion was not meant to stop when the revelation was completed."[160]

It must however be noted that those changes occurred within the context of an established order within the Arabian peninsula at the time of the revelation that was patriarchal. It was a culture with an andocentric bias, one where the male and the male experience are looked upon as the norm.

This was a society where it was not the norm for a woman to be educated, hold political power, to be involved in financial transactions or to be the primary or co-economic contributor in a family. The bias against woman was so strong that female infanticide was common.[161]

While patriarchy was clearly a specific cultural norm in 7th century Arabia and indeed, many parts of the world, it can in no way be considered universal. In fact, we have an example from history where a matrilineal culture was accommodated within an Islamic framework. Ibn Batuta visited Melle in 1352 and wrote:

> "My stay at Iwala-tan lasted about fifty days; and I was shown honor and entertained by its inhabitants. It is an excessively hot place, and boasts a few small date-palms, in the shade of which they sow watermelons. Its water comes from underground water's beds at that point, and there is plenty of mutton to be had. The garments of its inhabitants, most of whom belong to the Massufa tribe, are of fine Egyptian fabrics. Their women are of surpassing beauty, and are shown more respect than the men. The state of affairs amongst these people is indeed extraordinary. Their men show no signs of jealousy whatever; no one claims descent from his father, but on the contrary from his mother's brother. A person's heirs are his sister's sons, not his own sons. This is a thing which I have seen nowhere in the world except among the Indians of Malabar. But those are heathens; *these* people are Muslims, punctilious in observing the hours of prayer, studying books of law, and memorizing the Koran.[162]

In America and much of the West woman are fully engaged in every aspect of society. Surely, an Islamic approach can be developed in this cultural context as the Qur'an makes clear that humans were all created from the same soul, and the Prophet himself stated that women are the split halves of men.[163] A major juristic rule is that Islamic rulings change with the change of time and place [164] and Black woman have been on the front line of every aspect of Black Strivings from the beginning.

To the point, W.E.B. DuBois trusted black woman politically and socially and argued that the historical consequences of the Black female experience had created a specially equipped community of woman, an "efficient womanhood" that challenged the dominant culture's prescriptions for woman.[165] For all the fanfare generated by the Million Man March in 1995, my wife quipped, "We see the Million **Woman** March everyday; that is Black woman getting up and going to work!" The discussion for a relevant Islam must account for the contemporary role of woman in society.

In addition to the external structure, Allah has provided a moral framework to develop a lifestyle and culture that is pleasing to Allah:

> **6:151** Say, "Come, I will recite what your Lord has prohibited to you. [He commands] that you not associate anything with Him, and to parents, good treatment, and do not kill your children out of poverty; We will provide for you and them. And do not approach immoralities – what is apparent of them and what is concealed. And do not kill the soul which Allah has forbidden [to be killed] except by [legal] right. This has He instructed you that you may use reason."
> **6:152** And do not approach the orphan's property except in a way that is best [i.e., intending improvement] until he reaches maturity. And give full measure and weight in justice. We do not charge any soul except [with that within] its capacity. And when you speak [i.e., testify], be just, even if [it concerns] a near relative. And the covenant of Allah fulfill. This has He instructed you that you may remember.
> **6:153** And, [moreover], this is My path, which is straight, so follow it; and do not follow [other] ways, for you will be separated from His way. This has He instructed you that you may become righteous.

There will always be Muslims that focus on rituals to the exclusion of the higher intents and purposes of Al-islam; presumably because the rituals alone will pave a Believers path to paradise. The Prophet Muhammad (PBUH), in his farewell sermon, said, "Beware of Satan, for the safety of your religion. He has lost all hope that he will ever be able to lead you astray in big things, so beware of following him in small things.[166]" While some Muslims interpret this admonition from the Prophet as a charge to focus on the "perfect" execution of every element of fiqh and ritual, I see this as a warning not to confuse rituals with the larger issues of Iman (faith). Further, Allah has identified that there will be a diversity of levels of practice and Iman in the Muslim community and that sincere Muslims will enter paradise by the will of Allah:

> **35:32** Then We caused to inherit the Book those We have chosen of Our servants; and among them is he who wrongs himself [i.e., sins], and among them is he who is moderate, and among them is he who is foremost in good deeds by permission of Allah. That [inheritance] is what is the great bounty.
> **35:33** [For them are] gardens of perpetual residence which they will enter. They will be adorned therein with bracelets of gold and pearls, and their garments therein will be silk.
> **35:34** And they will say, "Praise to Allah, who has removed from us [all] sorrow. indeed, our Lord is Forgiving and Appreciative t
> **35:35** He who has settled us in the home of duration [i.e., Paradise] out of His bounty. There touches us not in it any fatigue, and there touches us not in it weariness [of mind]."

I believe that with this framework as a platform and with a collective intention to continue to work for worthy causes with like minded people a healthy evolution of Al-Islam in the Black Community and America can be realized.

Dr. Sherman Jackson describes a segment of the Black American Muslim community he labeled "Independents".

He generally describes these Muslims as difficult to define, not necessarily opposed to any other Muslim group, not adherents to an ideological platform, nor do they hold a formal membership with any established group[167]. I believe that Muslims that fit this description will be a key component of evolution of Black American Islam.

I am a member of a small Muslim community in Southern Prince George's County Maryland called the Islamic Society of Southern Prince George's County Maryland. The Prophet Muhammad (PBUH) is reported to have said that if three are traveling one should be appointed as Imam[168]. The concept of traveling in the way of Allah both literally and spiritually is pervasive in the Qur'an and Sunnah of the Prophet Muhammad (PBUH).

There are numerous terms in the Qur'an - Sharia, Sirat Al Mustaqim, Sunnah (used exclusively in the Qur'an to apply to Allah's way),Tariqa, Sabil, Minhaj, – that have varying connotations of way, path and and/ or way. Accordingly, I accepted the sacred responsibility of serving as Imam of the ISSPGC from its initial founding in 2001 until 2008 as we all continued our respective travels along the paths of Allah all the while praying for a better understanding of Al-Islam.

There is nothing particularly special about us. We are husbands, wives, fathers, siblings, managers, educators, entrepreneurs, laborers, students and trades people. We do not collectively adhere to a particular school of thought on Al-Islam and have a variety of perspectives, that could be labeled, "Sunni", Sufi" "Shia'" and every combination in between.

What we all agree on is that there is no object of worship except Allah, Muhammad Ibn Abdullah (PBUH) is the final messenger to all of mankind and that the Holy Qur'an is the ultimate guidance for anyone seeking to improve their relationship with The Creator.

We strive to do our best to bring the most good in our families, personal and professional relationships and we seek to reach out to and positively engage the community. We have hosted community days and participate in the annual walkathon for the Oxon Hill Food Pantry[169]. The pantry is managed by the Interfaith Community Action Council, a local group. We participated with the family of the late Jakari Butler to coordinate Muslim and Christian funerals[170] for Jakari, a young brother in our community, who tragically, like so many of our young Black men was the victim of a senseless murder. [171]

One of the community's co-founders, Khalil Shadeed is the producer of an award winning television program, the Scholar's Chair[172]. Another of our members, Amir Muhammad, has established America's Islamic American Heritage Museum in Washington, DC[173]. I believe our community fits Dr. Jackson's description of "Independents" with one exception[174], we have taken the time and effort to establish a Masjid. I believe that the continued development of Black American Islam will necessarily include the development of communities like ours organized by individuals that fit this category of "Independent" Muslims. Allah has revealed:

> 9:18. The mosques of Allah are only to be maintained by those who believe in Allah and the Last Day and establish prayer and give zakh and do not fear except Allah, for it is expected that those will be of the [rightly] guided.

The relatively small size initially of some of these networks of communities is not an issue. It is a principle of Islamic theology that revival begins and ends with the few, not the many. One need look no further than the revolutions that have started around the world sparked initially by a few ordinary people using social media.

Allah has revealed in the Qur'an that if you obey most of those upon the earth, they will mislead you from the way of Allah.[175]   The Prophet Muhammad (PBUH) is reported to have said, "Islam initiated as something strange, and it would revert to its (old position) of being strange, so good tidings for the strangers."[176]   The traditional understanding of this hadith of the Prophet (PBUH) is that the "strangers" are few in number.

Conclusion

Allah is all encompassing[177], Allah's earth is spacious[178], there is no community on earth that is not fit for the worship of Allah alone[179] and the Masjids are for Allah[180]!

There is a parable in the Holy Qur'an regarding a good and bad tree.

> **14:24** Have you not considered how Allah presents an example, [making] a good word like a good tree, whose root is firmly fixed and its branches [high] in the sky?
> **14:25** It produces its fruit all the time, by permission of its Lord. And Allah presents examples for the people that perhaps they will be reminded.
> **14:26** And the example of a bad word is like a bad tree, uprooted from the surface of the earth, not having any stability.
> **14:27** Allah keeps firm those who believe, with the firm word, in worldly life and in the Hereafter. And Allah sends astray the wrongdoers. And Allah does what He wills.

For me, this parable reinforces the idea that healthy expressions of Al-Islam generally grow out of the foundation of a particular culture and experience. The basic unit of society being the family, I believe that focusing on the family will result in the development of a balanced[181], relevant Al-Islam that is of practical benefit to people since it is within the context of families and close social network that people are first socialized.

We all experience "The Next Wave" as we raise our children and attempt to provide guidance for them to be productive, responsible members of society. We should not consider for an instant raising our children by teaching them to belittle their own family history and culture and their place in that history.

Said another way, seeking to force an understanding of Al-Islam, based narrowly on the experiences of others and that does not consider time, place and circumstance is contrary the natural development of a Muslim people as evidenced by the Qur'an, Sunnah of the Prophet Muhammad (PBUH) and common sense.

> **10:100** And it is not for a soul [i.e., anyone] to believe except by permission of Allah, and He will place defilement[182] upon those who will not use reason.

I would like to end this essay by asking for Allah's blessings for the best of my intentions and forgiveness for any errors I have made. Accordingly, any ideas that are correct and relevant in this essay are from Allah, any errors are mine and I pray to Allah for forgiveness. I will end the essay with the following ayah from the Holy as a dua (supplication) for this effort.

34:48 Say: "Verily my Lord doth cast the (mantle of) Truth (over His servants) He that has full knowledge of (all) that is hidden."
34:49 Say: "The Truth has arrived and Falsehood neither creates anything new nor restores anything."
34:50 Say: "If I am astray I only stray to the loss of my own soul: but if I receive guidance it is because of the inspiration of my Lord to me: it is He Who hears all things

2:286 Allah does not charge a soul except [with that within] its capacity. It will have [the consequence of] what [good] it has gained, and it will bear [the consequence of] what [evil] it has earned. "Our Lord, do not impose blame upon us if we have forgotten or erred. Our Lord, and lay not upon us a burden like that which You laid upon those before us. Our Lord, and burden us not with that which we have no ability to bear.

And pardon us; and forgive us; and have mercy upon us. You are our protector, so give us victory over the disbelieving people.

Āmīn

Dawud Abdur-Rahman

The Dhikr Within the Dhikr of Authenticity

The Dhikr of Authenticity is grounded in the theological concepts contained in the Holy Qur'an and the Sunnah of the Prophet Muhammad (PBUH) with particular emphasis on Allah's names and attributes.

Allah has revealed in the Holy Qur'an regarding Remembrance:

13:28. Those who have believed and whose hearts are assured by the remembrance of Allah. Unquestionably, by the remembrance of Allah hearts are assured."

الَّذِينَ ءَامَنُواْ وَتَطْمَئِنُّ قُلُوبُهُم بِذِكْرِ اللهِ أَلاَ بِذِكْرِ اللهِ تَطْمَئِنُّ الْقُلُوبُ

38:1 Sad By the Qur'an containing reminder...

ص وَالْقُرْءَانِ ذِى الذِّكْرِ

20:124. And whoever turns away from My remembrance – indeed, he will have a depressed [i.e., difficult] life, and We will gather [i.e., raise] him on the Day of Resurrection blind."

وَمَنْ أَعْرَضَ عَن ذِكْرِى فَإِنَّ لَهُ مَعِيشَةً ضَنكاً وَنَحْشُرُهُ يَوْمَ الْقِيَمَةِ أَعْمَى

Accordingly, to remember Allah is to find assurance and further, Allah has instructed that the Qur'an contains and *is* The Reminder or Remembrance. The Arabic word that is translated "assurance" in ayah 13:28 above comes from the root word Taumana (طَمَنَ) which means quiet, rest securely in, or satisfied with[183].

While I am aware of rituals and practices such as reciting Allah's names while rubbing Dhikr beads or chanting Allah's names and attributes in a ritual dance that are identified as Dhikr, my understanding of Al-Islam places a premium on exhibiting Allah's attributes, to the best of any person's ability practically within their sphere of relationships and influence. A belief in One God that produces a healthy self love that motivates you to do good to all people and the entire creation *is* the remembrance of Allah in my view. Therefore, Allah has instructed us to remember and not to deny him:

> **2:152**. So remember Me; I will remember you. And be grateful to Me and do not deny Me.

فَاذْكُرُونِى أَذْكُرْكُمْ وَاشْكُرُواْ لِي وَلاَ تَكْفُرُونِ

My understanding of this guidance is that we should exemplify, to the best of our abilities, the best application of the meanings of Allah's attributes and the guidance in the Holy Qur'an exemplified by the Sunnah of the Prophet Muhammad (PBUH) and not to undercut or invalidate that professed belief with inconsistent actions.

Our beloved Prophet (PBUH) has related in a hadith qudsi:

> I am as My servant thinks I am. I am with him when he makes mention of Me. If he makes mention of Me to himself, I make mention of him to Myself; and if he makes mention of Me in an assembly, I make mention of him in an assembly better than it.

And if he draws near to Me an arm's length, I draw near to him a fathom's length. And if he comes to Me walking, I go to him at speed.

As we hasten to good deeds, Allah hastens to us and helps us to do his good work.

The Prophet Muhammad (PBUH) is also reported to have said:

Allah's Messenger (peace be upon him) said, "When you come upon the pastures of Paradise feed on them." On being asked what the pastures of Paradise were he replied that they were circles where Allah was remembered.

While the above hadith is likely to be traditionally understood to refer to Dhikr circles where ritual practices are conducted, I believe this could also be interpreted to be groups of people that are working together on just causes. A Muslim is encouraged to join in on good works.

Allah has revealed:

4:85. Whoever intercedes for a good cause will have a share [i.e., reward] therefrom; and whoever intercedes for an evil cause will have a portion [i.e., burden] therefrom. And ever is Allah, over all things, a Keeper

مَّن يَشْفَعْ شَفَاعَةً حَسَنَةً يَكُنْ لَّهُ نَصِيبٌ مِّنْهَا وَمَن يَشْفَعْ شَفَاعَةً سَيِّئَةً يَكُنْ لَّهُ كِفْلٌ مَّنْهَا وَكَانَ اللَّهُ عَلَى كُلِّ شَىْءٍ مُّقِيتاً

Allah has revealed that he is remembered by any of his names or attributes as Allah has the best names:

17:110. Say, "Call upon Allah or call upon the Most Merciful [ar-Rahman]. Whichever [name] you call – to Him belong the best names." And do not recite [too] loudly in your prayer or [too] quietly but seek between that an [intermediate] way.

قُلِ ادْعُواْ اللَّهَ أَوِ ادْعُواْ الرَّحْمَـنَ أَيًّا مَّا تَدْعُواْ فَلَهُ الأَسْمَآءَ الْحُسْنَى وَلاَ تَجْهَرْ بِصَلاَتِكَ وَلاَ تُخَافِتْ بِهَا وَابْتَغِ بَيْنَ ذَلِكَ سَبِيلاً

7:180. And to Allah belong the best names, so invoke Him by them. And leave [the company of] those who practice deviation concerning His names. They will be recompensed for what they have been doing.

وَلِلَّهِ الأَسْمَآءُ الْحُسْنَى فَادْعُوهُ بِهَا وَذَرُواْ الَّذِينَ يُلْحِدُونَ فِى أَسْمَـئِهِ سَيُجْزَوْنَ مَا كَانُواْ يَعْمَلُونَ

Therefore, as I composed the Dhikr of Authenticity, I did not believe that I had to use every one of Allah's names nor every principle identified in the Holy Qur'an in a compact Remembrance to convey a comprehensive understanding of Al-Islam.

Although neither all of Allah's attributes nor is every Islamic principle explicitly mentioned, I understand that all of Allah's names and Qur'anic principles are inherently included in the comprehensive understanding of the principle of Tauheed the Dhikr of Authenticity is intended to convey.   Further Allah has revealed:

2:115. And to Allah belongs the east and the west. So wherever you [might] turn, there is the Face of Allah. Indeed, Allah is all-Encompassing and Knowing.

وَلِلَّهِ الْمَشْرِقُ وَالْمَغْرِبُ فَأَيْنَمَا تُوَلُّوا فَثَمَّ وَجْهُ اللَّهِ إِنَّ اللَّهَ وَسِعٌ عَلِيمٌ

I believe good actions are the most authentic manifestation of the belief in Al-Islam.

5:35. O you who have believed, fear Allah and seek the means [of nearness] to Him and strive in His cause that you may succeed.

يَا أَيُّهَا الَّذِينَ ءَامَنُوا اتَّقُوا اللَّهَ وَابْتَغُوا إِلَيْهِ الْوَسِيلَةَ وَجَاهِدُوا فِى سَبِيلِهِ لَعَلَّكُمْ تُفْلِحُونَ

Following is a line by line explanation of the Dhikr within The Dhikr of Authenticity.

Whoever you are... **BE IT!**

Proclaims Allah's purposefully creative powers. To be a Muslim is to accept the specific circumstances of your creation. However it is not to be understood that unfavorable situations cannot be improved through faith and your own effort. For instance, someone may have been born into a family where no one has ever attained a level of education beyond a high school diploma. That should not be used as an excuse to try to not strive for higher levels of education.

Allah has multiple names reflecting his creative powers. Each name carries a particular aspect of Allah's creative abilities. They are:

- Al-Khaliq, The Creator;
- Al-Bari, The Inventor;
- Al-Musawwir, The Fashioner
- Al-Badi, The Originator
- Al-Khallaq, The Creator
- Al-Fatir, The Creator

59:24. He is Allah, the Creator [Al-Khaliq], the Inventor [Al-Bari], the Fashioner [Al-Musawwir]; to Him belong the best names. Whatever is in the heavens and earth is exalting Him. And He is the Exalted in Might, the Wise.

هُوَ اللَّهُ الْخَلِقُ الْبَارِىءُ الْمُصَوِّرُ لَهُ الأَسْمَآءُ
الْحُسْنَى يُسَبِّحُ لَهُ مَا فِى السَّمَوَتِ وَالأَّرْضِ
وَهُوَ الْعَزِيزُ الْحَكِيمُ

2:117. Originator [Al-Badi] of the heavens and the earth. When He decrees a matter, He only says to it, "Be," and it is.

بَدِيعُ السَّمَـوَتِ وَالأَرْضِ وَإِذَا قَضَى أَمْرًا فَإِنَّمَا يَقُولُ لَهُ كُنْ فَيَكُونُ

15:86. Indeed, your Lord – He is the Knowing Creator [Al-Khallaq].

إِنَّ رَبَّكَ هُوَ الْخَلَّقُ الْعَلِيمُ

35:1. [All] praise is [due] to Allah, Creator [Al-Fatir] of the heavens and the earth, [who] made the angels messengers having wings, two or three or four. He increases in creation what He wills. Indeed, Allah is over all things competent.

الْحَمْدُ للهِ فَاطِرِ السَّمَـوَتِ وَالأَرْضِ جَاعِلِ الْمَلَـئِكَةِ رُسُلاً أُولِى أَجْنِحَةٍ مَّثْنَى وَثُلَـثَ وَرُبَـعَ يَزِيدُ فِى الْخَلْقِ مَا يَشَآءُ إِنَّ اللهَ عَلَى كُلِّ شَىْءٍ قَدِيرٌ

Al-Khaliq, The Creator;

> Al-Khaliq is an attribute of Allah. This name is derived from the word Khalaq which means to produce, to make, to assign, to access and to bring into existence from non-existence. Allah is the only One Who has created the heavens and the earth, Who has created all things in pairs and Who has knowledge of the nature of all the creations and exact stage of their making and production. He has divided all material and abstract things into different kinds, categories and shapes. Allah is the one being Who will remain forever, and I Whom all these qualities besides many others are manifested to ten utmost, and he is called Al-Khaliq.[184]

73

Al-Bari, The Inventor;

Baraa implies a process of evolving from previously created matter or state: the Author of the process is Bari-u. The Evolver and Maker. Allah is Al-Bari' because He creates all things in proportion. He is the Molder of each form and frame. He is the designer, Builder of Earth and Heavens. He has fashioned His angels and made them messengers. Verily He is Mighty. None can withhold what betoweth and none what he witholdeth. [185]

Al-Musawwir, The Fashioner

Sawwara implies giving definite form or color, so as to make a thing exactly suited to a given ebd or object: hence the title Musawwir, Bestower or Forms or colors i.e.: The fashioner. Allah is Al-Musawwir, because he designs all things. [186]

Al-Badi, The Originator

Al-Badi' is one of the ninety-nine special Attributes of Allah. It means 'He who originates." Allah creates wonders in the universe without any design. [187]

Al-Khallaq, The Creator

Al-Khallaq is one of the ninety-nine Attributes of Allah. Khallaq: the emphatic form, as meaning the Creator, Who is perfect in his skill and Knowledge, and whose creation answers perfectly to His design. Therefore, no one should think that anything has gone wrong in Allah's creation. What may seem out of joint is merely the result of our shortsighted standards, It often happens that what appears to us to be evil or imperfect or unjust is a reflection of our own imperfect mind.

Al-Fatir, The Creator

Al-Fatir is one of the ninety-nine Attributes of Allah which means 'The Creator"/ Allah is Fatir because he has created the heavens and the earth. Allah is Fatir because He is the Creator of nature and natural law. Allah is Fatir because nothing has gone wrong in His creation as he is perfect in His skill of creation. The word Fatir implies the creation of primeval matter, to which further creative processes have to be added by the hand of Allah, for Allah "adds to His Creations as he pleases", not only in quantity, but in qualities, functions, relations, and variations in infinite ways. Allah's creation did not stop at some past time: it continues for He has all power, and His mercies are ever poured forth without stint.

Allah created everything with purpose. Allah is:

Al-Qadir, The Able

Al-Qadir is an Attribute of Allah which manifests His power. His power is eternal a priori and posterirori. It is not posterior to His essence.[188]

Al-Muqtadir, The Powerful

Al-Muqtadir is an Attribute of Allah which is synonymous to His attribute Qadir.

The names of these attributes are derived from the Arabic root word "Qadara" a word who's meanings include; to be able to do, have power over, prevail, measure to an exact nicety estimate exactly, be sparing, determine, decree, grown, arrange, prepare, allot, devise, depose, appreciate, honor, assign, know, understand, straighten[189].

6:65. Say, "He is the [one] Able [Al-Qadir] to send upon you affliction from above you or from beneath your feet or to confuse you [so you become] sects and make you taste the violence of one another." Look how We diversify the signs that they might understand.

قُلْ هُوَ الْقَادِرُ عَلَى أَن يَبْعَثَ عَلَيْكُمْ عَذَاباً مِّن فَوْقِكُمْ أَوْ مِن
تَحْتِ أَرْجُلِكُمْ أَوْ يَلْبِسَكُمْ شِيَعاً وَيُذِيقَ بَعْضَكُم بَأْسَ بَعْضٍ
انْظُرْ كَيْفَ نُصَرِّفُ الآيَّتِ لَعَلَّهُمْ يَفْقَهُونَ

54:42. They denied Our signs, all of them, so We seized them with a seizure of one Exalted in Might and Perfect in Ability [Muqtadir]
:

كَذَّبُواْ بِـَايَـٰتِنَا كُلِّهَا فَأَخَذْنَـٰهُمْ أَخْذَ عِزِيزٍ مُّقْتَدِرٍ

Whatever good inspires you….STRIVE FOR IT!

Allah wants our strivings with might and main to be purposeful and for doing good.

29:69 And those who strive [jihad] in Our (Cause) We will certainly guide them to Our Paths [sabil]: for verily Allah is with those who do right [muhsineen].

وَالَّذِينَ جَـٰهَدُواْ فِينَا لَنَهْدِيَنَّهُمْ سُبُلَنَا وَإِنَّ اللَّهَ لَمَعَ
الْمُحْسِنِينَ

The root word for jihad means, to toil, exert strenuously, overload (a camel), be diligent, struggle, strive after, meditate upon a thing, struggle against difficulties, strive with might.[190]

Striving in the path of Allah means to diligently strive with every spiritual, physical, psychological resource available for good causes.

The muhsineen are those that behave righteously and are righteous people. I understand doing good comprehensively to include acts of justice, forgiveness, compassion, wisdom, generosity, patience, responsibility, etc...

29:6. And whoever strives only strives for [the benefit of] himself. Indeed, Allah is Free from need of the worlds.

وَمَن جَاهَدَ فَإِنَّمَا يُجَاهِدُ لِنَفْسِهِ إِنَّ اللَّهَ لَغَنِىٌّ عَنِ الْعَلَمِينَ

RESPOND to the Call to Life;

Allah is Al-Hayy, The Alive
Al-Hayy is an Attribute of Allah which means the Ever-Living, the Deathless, the Eternal. His existence having neither beginning nor end.[191]

3:2. Allah – there is no deity except Him, the Ever-Living, the Sustainer of existence.

اللَّهُ لَا إِلَهَ إِلَّا هُوَ الْحَيُّ الْقَيُّومُ

8:24. O you who have believed, respond to Allah and to the Messenger when he calls you to that which gives you life. And know that Allah intervenes between a man and his heart and that to Him you will be gathered.

يَأَيُّهَا الَّذِينَ ءَامَنُوا اسْتَجِيبُوا لِلَّهِ وَلِلرَّسُولِ إِذَا دَعَاكُمْ لِمَا يُحْيِيكُمْ وَاعْلَمُوا أَنَّ اللَّهَ يَحُولُ بَيْنَ الْمَرْءِ وَقَلْبِهِ وَأَنَّهُ إِلَيْهِ تُحْشَرُونَ

45:18. Then We put you, [O Muhammad], on an ordained way [sharia] concerning the matter [of religion]; so follow it and do not follow the inclinations of those who do not know.

ثُمَّ جَعَلْنَاكَ عَلَى شَرِيعَةٍ مِّنَ الأَمْرِ فَاتَّبِعْهَا وَلاَ تَتَّبِعْ أَهْوَآءَ الَّذِينَ لاَ يَعْلَمُونَ

In *The Spirit of Islamic Law*, Professor Bernard G. Weiss states "In archaic Arabic, the term shar.'a means 'path to the water hole ' When we consider the importance of a well-trodden path to a source of water for man and beast in the arid desert environment, we can readily appreciate why this term in Muslim usage should have become a metaphor for a whole way of life ordained by God. [192] I understand Al-Islam is literally, spiritually and metaphysically the way the leads to life, not stagnation or death, in this world and in the hereafter.

With a Humble Certainty;

Allah is Al-Kabir, The Greatest.
Al-Kabir is a Name of Allah coming from Kibr which means greatness, haughtiness, pride and dignity. It implies that He is Most Dignified and Greatest. He is the One and the Only Being, Whose existence is free of time and place. He is existing from Eternity and will remain forever to Eternity.

He is the Creator and Sustainer of all creations, worlds, heavens and earth including all those places which were shown to the Holy Prophet Muhammad (peace and blessings of Allah be upon him). He knows all things, acts and facts open or hidden anywhere, and He is Lofty and above everything in Divinity.

His grandeur and greatness will be shown on the Great Day, when He will shower immense blessings on His obedient servants, and they will be rewarded profusely. He is pure and free of all evils, vices, defects, sexes, blemishes and necessities. The Holy Prophet Muhammad (peace and blessings of Allah be upon him) has prescribed the following prayer for our recitation:

> O Allah! Make me small in my own eyes and great in the eyes of other people.[193]

Allah is Al-Kabir, The Greatest

34:23. And intercession does not benefit with Him except for one whom He permits. [And those wait] until, when terror is removed from their hearts, they will say [to one another], "What has your Lord said?" They will say, "The truth." And He is the Most High, the Grand.

وَلاَ تَنفَعُ الشَّفَـعَةُ عِندَهُ إِلاَّ لِمَنْ أَذِنَ لَهُ حَتَّى إِذَا فُزِّعَ عَن قُلُوبِهِمْ قَالُواْ مَاذَا قَالَ رَبُّكُمْ قَالُواْ الْحَقَّ وَهُوَ الْعَلِىُّ الْكَبِيرُ

Allah is Al-Adheem, The Most Great

> Allah is called Al-Adheem as He is above everything in Divinity, and also as He is the One and only Being, who will remain forever. There is no god save Him, the Ever-Living, the Eternal.

He is the Creator of the great heavens, the Most Bounteous, the Greatest of all.

Unto Him belongeth whatsoever is on the earth. His throne overspends the heavens and the earth. He is the Maker of kings, the Savior of all beings from trials and tribulations, and He gives honor and power to whom He likes.

He has bestowed the Holy Qur'an on His servants for their guidance and salvation. He brings all the creations into existence from non-existence. He guides His obedient servants to success and salvation in the eternal life. [194]

2:255. Allah – there is no deity except Him, the Ever-Living, the Sustainer of [all] existence. Neither drowsiness overtakes Him nor sleep. To Him belongs whatever is in the heavens and whatever is on the earth. Who is it that can intercede with Him except by His permission? He knows what is [presently] before them and what will be after them, and they encompass not a thing of His knowledge except for what He wills. His Kursi extends over the heavens and the earth, and their preservation tires Him not. And He is the Most High, the Most Great.

اللّهُ لاَ إِلَـهَ إِلاَّ هُوَ الْحَىُّ الْقَيُّومُ لاَ تَأْخُذُهُ سِنَةٌ وَلاَ نَوْمٌ لَّهُ مَا فِي السَّمَـوَاتِ وَمَا فِي الأَرْضِ مَن ذَا الَّذِى يَشْفَعُ عِندَهُ إِلاَّ بِإِذْنِهِ يَعْلَمُ مَا بَيْنَ أَيْدِيهِمْ وَمَا خَلْفَهُمْ وَلاَ يُحِيطُونَ بِشَيْءٍ مِّنْ عِلْمِهِ إِلاَّ بِمَا شَاءَ وَسِعَ كُرْسِيُّهُ السَّمَـوَاتِ وَالأَرْضَ وَلاَ يَؤُودُهُ حِفْظُهُمَا وَهُوَ الْعَلِىُّ الْعَظِيمُ

Because of the unqualified greatness of Allah, humility is an important quality in Al-Islam and Allah does not favor those that are arrogant.

25:63. And the servants of the Most Merciful are those who walk upon the earth easily, and when the ignorant address them [harshly], they say [words of] peace

وَعِبَادُ الرَّحْمَنِ الَّذِينَ يَمْشُونَ عَلَى الْأَرْضِ هَوْناً وَإِذَا خَاطَبَهُمُ الْجَـٰهِلُونَ قَالُواْ سَلاَماً

Muslims imbibe the quality Yaqeen; certainty. Muslims are buoyed by the certainty of the faith that never allows even an inkling of doubt.

2:4. And who believe in what has been revealed to you, [O Muhammad], and what was revealed before you, and of the Hereafter **they are certain** [in faith].

وَالَّذِينَ يُؤْمِنُونَ بِمَآ أُنزِلَ إِلَيْكَ وَمَآ أُنزِلَ مِن قَبْلِكَ وَبِالأَخِرَةِ هُمْ يُوقِنُونَ

102:5 No! If you only knew with knowledge of certainty...

كَلاَّ لَوْ تَعْلَمُونَ عِلْمَ الْيَقِينِ

Grounded in Love and a Reasoning Faith;

Allah is Al-Wudud – The Love
> Wadud is another Attribute of Allah. It means that Entity which is loved, adored and worshipped.

81

His obedient servants love Him and he loves them. Undoubtedly, love is from both sides. It is initiated by Allah and reciprocated by His servants.[195]

11:90. And ask forgiveness of your Lord and then repent to Him. Indeed, my Lord is Merciful and Most Loving[196]."

وَاسْتَغْفِرُواْ رَبَّكُمْ ثُمَّ تُوبُواْ إِلَيْهِ إِنَّ رَبِّى رَحِيمٌ وَدُودٌ

Allah loves those that follow the example of the Prophet Muhammad (PBUH)

3:31 Say, [O Muhammad], "If you should love Allah, then follow me,[so] Allah will love you and forgive you your sins. And Allah is Forgiving and Merciful."

قُلْ إِن كُنتُمْ تُحِبُّونَ اللَّهَ فَاتَّبِعُونِى يُحْبِبْكُمُ اللَّهُ وَيَغْفِرْ لَكُمْ ذُنُوبَكُمْ وَاللَّهُ غَفُورٌ رَّحِيمٌ

The revelation of the Qur'an is for those that use reason

2:242. Thus does Allah make clear to you His verses [i.e., laws] that you might use reason.

كَذَلِكَ يُبَيِّنُ اللَّهُ لَكُمْ آيَـتِهِ لَعَلَّكُمْ تَعْقِلُونَ

8:22. Indeed, the worst of living creatures in the sight of Allah are the deaf and dumb who do not use reason [i.e., the disbelievers].

إِنَّ شَرَّ الدَّوَابِّ عِندَ اللّٰهِ الصُّمُّ الْبُكْمُ الَّذِينَ لاَ يَعْقِلُونَ

Reinforced by the Peace of a Patient Steadfastness;

Allah is As-Salaam – The Peace

Salam is the proper name for Allah. It means security in its entirety, free from any hazard and decline. The name Salam manifests that all His obedient servants are protected and endowed with security by Him. When the angel Jibra'il conveyed greetings from Allah and from himself to Hadrat Khadijah (Allah be pleased with her) wife of the Messenger of Allah (peace and blessings be upon him), she said in reply that they get security from Almighty Allah alone. Deen with Allah is Al-Islam. Islam is the name of the Religion selected and favored by Allah its meaning being to bow down before Him. It is closely related with the name Salam.[197]

59:23 He is Allah, other than whom there is no deity, the Sovereign, the Pure, the Perfection [As-Salaam] , the Bestower of Faith, the Overseer, the Exalted in Might, the Compeller, the Superior, Exalted is Allah above whatever they associate with Him.

هُوَ اللّٰهُ الَّذِى لاَ إِلَـهَ إِلاَّ هُوَ الْمَلِكُ الْقُدُّوسُ السَّلَـمُ الْمُؤْمِنُ الْمُهَيْمِنُ الْعَزِيزُ الْجَبَّارُ الْمُتَكَبِّرُ سُبْحَـنَ اللّٰهِ عَمَّا يُشْرِكُونَ

Allah loves the Patient

2:153. O you who have believed, seek help through patience and prayer. Indeed, Allah is with the patient.

يَـٰٓأَيُّهَا الَّذِينَ ءَامَنُواْ اسْتَعِينُواْ بِالصَّبْرِ وَالصَّلَوٰةِ إِنَّ اللَّهَ مَعَ الصَّـٰبِرِينَ

11:115. And be patient, for indeed, Allah does not allow to be lost the reward of those who do good.

وَاصْبِرْ فَإِنَّ اللَّهَ لَا يُضِيعُ أَجْرَ الْمُحْسِنِينَ

3:200 O you who have believed, persevere and endure and remain stationed and fear Allah that you may be successful.

يَـٰٓأَيُّهَا الَّذِينَ ءَامَنُواْ اصْبِرُواْ وَصَابِرُواْ وَرَابِطُواْ وَاتَّقُواْ اللَّهَ لَعَلَّكُمْ تُفْلِحُونَ

And Preserved by a Vigilant Consciousness regarding your Relationship with Allah (God) and the Creation

Allah is Al-Hafiz, the Protector.
Al-Hafiz is one of the ninety-nine attributes of Allah which means 'the Protector" The Holy Qur'an is the Word of Allah and He is preserving it; therefore no one can do any harm to it; nor can discredit it by its ridicules, taunts and objections; nor can hamper progress, whatever he may do against it; nor will anyone be ever able to change or tamper with it. [198]

Therefore we should be protective of our relationship with Allah, with ourselves and with each other.

11:57. But if they turn away, [say], "I have already conveyed that with which I was sent to you. My Lord will give succession to a people other than you, and you will not harm Him at all. Indeed my Lord is, over all things, Guardian."

فَإِن تَوَلَّوْاْ فَقَدْ أَبْلَغْتُكُم مَّآ أُرْسِلْتُ بِهِ إِلَيْكُمْ وَيَسْتَخْلِفُ رَبِّى قَوْمًا غَيْرَكُمْ وَلاَ تَضُرُّونَهُ شَيْئًا إِنَّ رَبِّى عَلَى كُلِّ شَىْءٍ حَفِيظٌ

Allah is also guardian of the Holy Qur'an:

15:9. Indeed, it is We who sent down the message [i.e., the Qur'an],
and indeed, We will be its guardian.

إِنَّا نَحْنُ نَزَّلْنَا الذِّكْرَ وَإِنَّا لَهُ لَحَفِظُونَ

There are many people, Muslim and non-Muslim that make false claims and undertake unjust actions in the name of "Islam". Allah has revealed:

61:7. And who is more unjust than one who invents about Allah untruth while he is being invited to Islam. And Allah does not guide the wrongdoing people.
61:8. They want to extinguish the light of Allah with their mouths, but Allah will perfect His light, although the disbelievers dislike it.
61:9. It is He who sent His Messenger with guidance and the religion of truth to manifest it over all religion, although those who associate others with Allah dislike it.

وَمَنْ أَظْلَمُ مِمَّنِ افْتَرَى عَلَى اللهِ الْكَذِبَ وَهُوَ يُدْعَى إِلَى الإِسْلاَمِ وَاللَّهُ لاَ يَهْدِى الْقَوْمَ الظَّالِمِينَ - يُرِيدُونَ لِيُطْفِئُوا نُورَ اللَّهِ بِأَفْوَاهِهِمْ وَاللَّهُ مُتِمُّ نُورِهِ وَلَوْ كَرِهَ الْكَفِرُونَ - هُوَ الَّذِى أَرْسَلَ رَسُولَهُ بِالْهُدَى وَدِينِ الْحَقِّ لِيُظْهِرَهُ عَلَى الدِّينِ كُلِّهِ وَلَوْ كَرِهَ الْمُشْرِكُونَ

Allah urges taqwa, word meaning God-fearing, devout[199] that includes a pervasive consciousness, awe and fear. The Qur'an uses this term repeatedly and says the Qur'an is guidance for those that have this quality.

9:4...Indeed, Allah loves the righteous [who fear Him].

إِنَّ اللَّهَ يُحِبُّ الْمُتَّقِينَ

2:2. This is the Book about which there is no doubt, a guidance for those conscious of Allah

ذَلِكَ الْكِتَابُ لاَ رَيْبَ فِيهِ هُدًى لِّلْمُتَّقِينَ

24:52. And whoever obeys Allah and His Messenger and fears Allah and is conscious of Him – it is those who are the attainers.

وَمَن يُطِعِ اللَّهَ وَرَسُولَهُ وَيَخْشَ اللَّهَ وَيَتَّقْهِ فَأُوْلَئِكَ هُمُ الْفَائِزُونَ

Allah is the proper name applied to the Being who exists necessarily, by Himself, comprising all the attributes of perfection.[200]

> **20:14**. Indeed, I am Allah. There is no deity except Me, so worship Me and establish prayer for My remembrance..

إِنَّنِى أَنَا اللهُ لا إِلَـٰهَ إِلا أَنَا فَاعْبُدْنِى وَأَقِمِ الصَّلَوةَ لِذِكْرِى

Allah is the Creator and Sustainer whose will reigns supreme in the universe and who alone is worthy of the highest honor, the greatest respect and admiration and is the sole object of worship. The word is in fact incapable of translation and the other words like God, Deity are poor substitutes for it. It is not a common noun meaning a god or a divine being. It is a proper noun par excellence.

No plural can be derived from it and it has, according to the best authorities, no root and derivation. The word connotes all attributes of perfection and beauty in their infinitude and denotes none but the One and Unique God, the Supreme, Perfect, Tender, Mighty and Most Gracious, Most Benign and Compassionate.

The title Allah is called the Ism az-Zat, or the essential name of God, all other titles including Rabb (Lord), being considered Asma' as-Sifat, or "attributes" of the Divine Being. The attributes are called al-Asma' al-Husna or the "Excellent Names."[201]

Correct belief in Allah is of paramount importance in al-Islam. In a sahih hadith, the Prophet (PBUH) told one of his companions who was riding behind him on a camel that belief in Allah is all that is required to enter paradise. The companion asked if he should tell everyone. The Prophet (PBUH) said "No", because he did not want people to sit idle[202].

I understand the guidance of the Prophet Muhammad (PBUH) as reinforcing the imperative in Al-Islam for faith and action.

Finally, Allah has placed the responsibility of governance of the creation on human beings as he has called mankind to be Khalifah. The root meaning of the word Khalifah means, to be behind, come after, to succeed. It carries the meanings, a successor, lieutenant vicar.[203]

> **2: 30**. And [mention, O Muhammad], when your Lord said to the angels, "Indeed, I will make upon the earth [Al-Ard] a successive authority." They said, "Will You place upon it one who causes corruption therein and sheds blood, while we declare Your praise and sanctify You?" He [Allah] said, "Indeed, I know that which you do not know."

وَإِذْ قَالَ رَبُّكَ لِلْمَلَـئِكَةِ إِنِّي جَاعِلٌ فِى الأَرْضِ خَلِيفَةً قَالُواْ
أَتَجْعَلُ فِيهَا مَن يُفْسِدُ فِيهَا وَيَسْفِكُ الدِّمَآءَ وَنَحْنُ نُسَبِّحُ بِحَمْدِكَ
وَنُقَدِّسُ لَكَ قَالَ إِنِّي أَعْلَمُ مَا لاَ تَعْلَمُونَ

In the Arabic language, the root provides the basic lexical meaning of the word.[204] The lexical root word for the Arabic word, Earth, Ard (ارض)has the following meanings according to Lanes Lexicon:

> It became pleasing to the eye, and disposed by nature to yield good produce; it became fruitful and in good condition; it collected moisture and became luxuriat with herbage; it became soft to tread upon, productive and in good in its vegetation[205].

When adding the definite article "Al", in Arabic for The Earth (الارض), the Arabs understood and the Qur'anic understanding of Al-Ard includes:

That whereon are mankind; earth as opposed to heaven: and the ground, as meaning the surface of the earth, on which we tread and sit and lie. It is a feminine word[206].

That title Khalifah indicates the responsibility out of love for Allah and the creation to create a sustainable world where the diversity of Allah's creation is celebrated, nurtured and marshaled for the common good.

Āmīn

Dawud Abdur-Rahman

Dhikr to the Throw Back Negro

If we accept what we are taught
Black People
Never did
Never will
Don't deserve
Anything

But…

I Can't Be No Throwback Negro

Black People created
Kemet
Mesopotamia
Olmec
Harrapa
Great African and Afro-Asiatic Civilizations

But…

I Can't Be No Throw Back Negro

The Pan-Black Holocaust
Was Savage
Without precedent
Inexplicable
Irreconcilable
But…

I Can't Be No Throwback Negro

I
My Family
This Time
This Place
This Reality
Is Here
Now
So…

I Can't Be No Throwback Negro

Learn from the Past
From the Human Family
Propel to the Future
Embrace your starting point
By the Decree of Allah

Can't be No Throwback Negro

Know
Embrace
Appreciate
Respect
Love
Yourself

Submit to the Will of Allah

Don't Be No Throwback Negro

Dhikr to the Throwback Negro, an Essay

W.E.B. DuBois famously wrote:

> Here, then, is the dilemma, and it is a puzzling one, I admit. No Negro who has given earnest thought to the situation of his people in America has failed, at some time in life, to find himself at these cross-roads; has failed to ask himself at some time: What, after all, am I? Am I an American or am I a Negro? Can I be both? Or is it my duty to cease to be a Negro as soon as possible and be an American? If I strive as a Negro, am I not perpetuating the very cleft that threatens and separates Black and White America? Is not my only possible practical aim the subduction of all that is Negro in me to the American? Does my black blood place upon me any more obligation to assert my nationality than German, or Irish or Italian blood would?[207]

> After the Egyptian and Indian, the Greek and Roman, the Teuton and Mongolian, the Negro is a sort of seventh son, born with a veil, and gifted with second-sight in this American world, —a world which yields him no true self-consciousness, but only lets him see himself through the revelation of the other world. It is a peculiar sensation, this double-consciousness, this sense of always looking at one's self through the eyes of others, of measuring one's soul by the tape of a world that looks on in amused contempt and pity. One ever feels his twoness,—an American, a Negro; two souls, two thoughts, two unreconciled strivings; two warring ideals in one dark body, whose dogged strength alone keeps it from being torn asunder.

The history of the American Negro is the history
of this strife,— this longing to attain self-
conscious manhood, to merge his double self
into a better and truer self. In this merging he
wishes neither of the older selves to be lost. He
would not Africanize America, for America has
too much to teach the world and Africa. He
would not bleach his Negro soul in a flood of
white Americanism, for he knows that Negro
blood has a message for the world. He simply
wishes to make it possible for a man to be both a
Negro and an American, without being cursed
and spit upon by his fellows, without having the
doors of Opportunity closed roughly in his
face.[208]

The Dhikr to the Throw Back Negro is the companion piece,
and a book end to the Dhikr of Authenticity, The Essay. In
addition to "Remembrance" the Arabic word Dhikr also means
"Admonition". The lexical root meaning of the word means, "to
strike a man on the private parts"[209]. A Dhikr hits hard and
stays with you. When a person accepts Al-Islam, they testify
that there is no object of worship except Allah.

Muslims will often also accompany this declaration of faith with
a negation of disbelief; that in addition to the professed
affirmative belief that there is no object of adoration except
Allah they also *do not* disbelieve Allah. That is, Muslims are
on guard for beliefs and actions that negate and undermine
the positive affirmation of Allah as the sole object worthy of
adoration. In the construct of the Dhikr of Authenticity
philosophy, The Dhikr to the Throwback Negro is that negative
declaration. While the Dhikr of Authenticity affirms who you
are, the Dhikr to the Throwback Negro rejects a desire to
become someone else. It is an admonition.

It was inspired by an observation that I and my circle of friends have made regarding a phenomenon that develops in some Black people who for a variety of reasons seek to replace their culture and history with the culture and history of a past people. Sadly, these people, after studying Black History and comparing our history to the history of other people, have a difficult time accepting our history and consciously or unconsciously decide it is more appealing to become someone else.

Because of the preponderance of great Black civilizations of the past, some illogically conclude that Blackness and greatness are synonymous and transferable over time and space. Others might believe that another people have some special relationship with the divine that can only be shared by tapping into that culture. At its worse, their faith and cultural self worth are rooted exclusively in the experience of another people. Some don't necessarily reach back into history directly for identity, they appropriate another culture in whole or in part from another contemporary people.

The connection to these contemporary people then provides a vehicle to attach to another history and often leads to a misalignment of causes. A misalignment of causes occurs with people that are focused exclusively on issues in a Muslim community somewhere else; giving short shrift, or completely ignoring the plethora of issues in their own families and/ or communities.

In some ways people that reject their culture engage in a dysfunctional form of the Sufi concept of fana. Fana is a Sufi term for dissolution. It means to dissolve the self, while remaining physically alive. Persons having entered this enlightenment state obtain awareness of the intrinsical unity (Tauheed) between Allah and all that exists, including the individual's mind[210]. In the case of the Throwback Negro however, the individual dissolves their history and culture in favor of another one.

DuBois' classic concept of double consciousness has stood the test of time, is still quoted regularly and speaks to the particular dilemma of identity experienced by some people. In the extreme, this dilemma revolves around two unacceptable choices. The choice of being an American while not feeling completely or only marginally a part of American society or that of a Negro, the name used for a Black person during DuBois' time, thereby claiming membership in an enslaved, rejected race with no history or genius as presented from the perspective of White Supremacy. Malcolm X stated that because of disenfranchisement in American society, neither he, nor were any other Black People Americans[211].

James Baldwin went so far as to proclaim that "Negroes do not…exist in any other [country].[212] The fact that today there is even a proposal to consider that we have entered a post racial America speaks to the progress made on race relations in America however, for some it is bitter/ sweet and unsatisfying as the gains were not achieved though heroic physical revolt for instance like that of Spartacus or the fight by America for its independence from the British.

As Dr. Martin Luther King Jr. noted, 'the eye-for-an-eye philosophy, the impulse to defend oneself when attacked, has always been held as the highest measure of American manhood. We are a nation that worships the frontier tradition, and our heroes are those who champion justice through violent retaliation against injustice."[213] Today DNA testing is debunking the myth of many Blacks that they have 'Indian" blood, severing a connection to a people that are seen as having gone down swinging.[214]

The acceptance of Al-Islam can include a need to reconcile socio-cultural practices, identity and sincerity of faith. This acceptance involves a simultaneous introduction of a pure monotheism and the proposed acceptance of the manifestation of that monotheism within a range of cultural traditions traversing time and space that are often considered the norm for authentic expressions of Al-Islam.

This is an inherent part of the dynamics associated with the acceptance of Al-Islam due to the theological principle that a Muslim is a part of one ummah or community. Those established norms do not include the West generally, America specifically and can sometimes be in direct conflict with modernity. Robert Danin states, "the Islamic movement in the United States challenges the accepted conventions of social anthropology. Each time the anthropologist seems to have grasped the essence of a Muslim community defined in terms of shared religious principles – the Qur'an, the hadith, worship – this unity disintegrates under the pressures of personal interpretation, ethnic controversy, linguistic diversity, and even nationalist preoccupations. The resulting fragmentation in its turn then provokes an incessant reclassification of the other Muslim as well as endless crisis of identity.

The African American Muslim lives these contradictions as a series of compound statuses reminiscent of W.E.B. DuBois' theory of double-consciousness black and non-Christian, non-Arab and Muslim, indigenous American and religious convert, traditional Muslim woman and modern American feminist."[215] Personally, I see myself as a Black American that has embraced the five pillars of Al-Islam as my religious foundation.

For some that are still grappling with it, the identity question is resolved consciously or unconsciously by sidestepping and jettisoning Black American identity altogether by simply becoming someone else by embracing another culture and/ or history. There are a myriad of reasons why this solution could become plausible for some. Possibly tied to an unhealthy need for belonging stemming from unresolved family of origin issues. Placing the Hadith of the Prophet Muhammad (PBUH) on par with the Holy Qur'an is often a contributing factor. Salafi interpretations which tend to rely on faith alone rather than scientific reasoning or philosophy in questions of religion and ignore the space time-time differentials between the time of the Prophet Muhammad (PBUH) and modern America[216] represent an example of this type of approach to faith.

It should be noted however that this condition is not unique to Black American Muslims or to the incorporation of Al-Islam and can be seen in other ideologies. For instance Black American's historic attachment to the Hebrew's slavery in Egypt ultimately resulted in some groups accepting Black American slavery in America as a literal prophesy resulting in Blacks being the direct literal descendants of the biblical Black Hebrews[217].

A Muslim however is required to face reality squarely and to turn to Allah with a conscious striving. Black Americans are a distinct people with a distinct history that exists as a result of Allah's Qadr and therefore our history and culture is as authentic as anyone else's history. According to Islamic theology, all people, past and present, will be raised and judged based on their response to tests from Allah. It is a sensitive and complicated subject that warrants a focused discussion.

Frankly, identity and authenticity is a relevant larger conversation in America as individual's quest to find inner peace fuels an eleven billion dollar self improvement industry[218]. What is pertinent as a starting point in this piece from my perspective for a Muslim is what Allah has revealed in the Holy Qur'an on the matter. The Qur'an and Sunnah are clear that all people are created by the will of Allah and that we have the opportunity to draw nearer to Allah through faith and good deeds. Allah informs us to review the deeds of former people, and to understand that all people, past and current will one day be raised by Allah for judgment.

Allah has created us into people and tribes.

> **49:13** O mankind, indeed We have created you from male and female and made you peoples and tribes that you may know one another. Indeed, the most noble of you in the sight of Allah is the most righteous of you. Indeed, Allah is Knowing and Acquainted.

At the same time Muslims are considered one community, the Prophet Muhammad (PBUH) acknowledged the various tribes that make up the community and ordered the building of masjids in the areas of each of the tribes.

The Apostle of Allah (peace be upon him) commanded us to build mosques in different localities (i.e. in the locality of each tribe separately) and that they should be kept clean and be perfumed.

Allah instructs us to study people of former times:

> **35:44** Have they not traveled through the land and observed how was the end of those before them? And they were greater than them in power. But Allah is not to be caused failure [i.e., prevented] by anything in the heavens or on the earth. Indeed, He is ever Knowing and Competent.

Allah has sent messengers to previous people:

> **15:10** And We had certainly sent [messengers] before you, [O Muhammad], among the sects of the former peoples.
>
> **56:49** Say, [O Muhammad], "Indeed, the former and later peoples
> **56:50** Are to be gathered together for the appointment of a known Day."

I understand us to be "later" people, in a particular time, place and circumstance. I believe we need to "Lower our Buckets", as Booker T. Washington exhorted and to be ourselves, and not another as W.E.B. DuBois asserted by turning to Allah by embracing ourselves and away from false worship.

Allah knows best.

Āmīn

Dawud Abdur-Rahman

A Dhika to the Hataz[219]

Among the definitions in the Urban dictionary for Hataz[220] are:

1. A person, or group of people who hate on what you have.
2. Another word for jealousy.
3. Talking bad about someone for no reason at all.

The fact of the matter is that anyone that ventures on the inner journey of self actualization and who has the courage to live authentically in a manner that is pleasing to themselves and Allah is **guaranteed** to attract Hataz. Hataz will come from shocking places and from family and friends you never imagined would ever say or do anything intentionally to harm you. These are people who envy. The Arabic word for envy is hasad. These people envy not because of anything you may have done to them, but because of inadequacies they do not have the courage to face within themselves.

We know this personality and dynamic. Black culture has produced a slew of classic songs in every phase of our experience about these people. These songs transcendent time, we know them. Songs like:

- Smiling Faces (The Undisputed Truth);
- Backstabbers (The O'Jays);
- Hate on me (Jill Scott);
- Vapors (Biz Markie)
- Etc...

The Prophet Muhammad (PBUH) in one of his hadith has advised:

Islam initiated as something strange, and it would revert to its (old position) of being strange, so good tidings for the strangers."[221] The traditional understanding of this hadith is that the Islam began with a few individuals and it will return to a few individuals. In addition to the traditional understanding, I also understand it to mean, at the end of the day, with the multitude of friends and relationships that come and go during a lifetime, there will only be a handful of truly quality relationships that were truly authentic and real and mutually healthy and that result is a state of peace, safety and security; Al-Islam.

Allah subpanna wata Allah revealed in the 113th chapter of the Holy Qur'an the following ayah specifically to address these individuals. Allah has revealed:

113:1. Say, "I seek refuge in the Lord of daybreak
113:2. From the evil of that which He created
113:3. And from the evil of darkness when it settles
113:4. And from the evil of the blowers in knots
113:5. And from the evil of an envier when he envies."

Remember this surah, it will help, you. If you embark on the greater jihad to defeat your base desires, fears self perceived inadequacies.....you will need it.

Allah knows best.

Āmīn

About the Author

Dawud Abdur-Rahman is a family-oriented man who is married with 3 children and one grandson. Born and raised in Philadelphia, Pennsylvania, he now lives in Maryland suburbs of the Washington, DC.

Dawud holds a Bachelor of Business Administration from Temple University and a Master of Business Administration from Averett College. His graduate research project explored Spirituality in the Workplace.

Dawud is interested in Islamic Spirituality and served as Imam for the Islamic Society of Prince George's County from its founding in 2002 until 2008. He appears regularly on The Scholar's Chair television program and participates regularly in Interfaith discussions and activities.

Dawud Abdur-Rahman

Bibliography

'Abd al 'Ati, Hammudah. Islam in Focus. Amana Publications, 1418/ 1998

al Faruqi, Abdur-Rahman, Dawud, A Study of Spirituality in the Workplace. A Research Paper Submitted in Candidacy for the Degree of Master of Business Administration, Averett College. September 23, 1999

al-Jerrahi al-Halveti Bayrak, Sheik Tosun, The Most Beautiful Names, Threshold Books, 1985

Isma'il Raji, Tawhid, Its Relevance For Thought and Life. I.I.F.S.O., 1983

Bell, Berbard W.; Grosholtz, Emily R.; Stewart, James B., W.E.B. DuBois On Race & Culture. Routledge, 1996

Cosby, Bill and Poussaint M.D., Alvin F., Come On People, On the Path From Victims to Victors. Thomas Nelson, 2007

Curtis IV, Edward E., Islam in Black America. State University of New York Press, 2002

Dannin, Robert, Black Pilgrimage to Islam. Oxford University Press, 2002

DuBois, W.E.B.. Dusk of Dawn, An Essay Toward An Autobiography of A Race Concept. Transaction Publishers, 1984

DuBois, W.E.B., The Study of the Negro Problems, 1898

DuBois, W.E.B. The Souls of Black Folk. Simon and Schuster, Inc. 2005

DuBois, W.E.B, The World and Africa, An Inquiry into the part which Africa has played in World History. International Publishers, New York. 1965

Dyson, Michael Eric, Is Bill Cosby Right (Or Has The Black Middle Class Lost Its Mind), Basic Civitas Books 2006

DuBois, W.E.B., Development of a People, 1904

Du Bois, *W.E.B, The Negro* and *The Conservation of Races* by, the Pennsylvania State University, *Electronic Classics Series*, Jim Manis, Faculty Editor, Hazleton, PA 18202-1291 is a Portable Document File produced as part of an ongoing student publication project to bring classical works of literature, in English, to free and easy access of those wishing to make use of them. Cover Design: Jim Manis Copyright © 2007 The Pennsylvania State University

DuBois, W.E.B. The Strivings of the Negro People, 1897
Esposito, John I., The Future of Islam. Oxford University Press, 2010

Gates Jr., Henry Louis/ West, Cornel, The Future of the Race. Vantage Books, 1996

Gayraud, William S., Black Religion and Black Radicalism, An Interpretation of the Religious History of African Americans. Orbis Books, 1998

Haddad, Yvonne Yazbeck and Esposito, John L., Muslims on the Americanization Path?. Oxford University Press, 1998

Harris, Rabia, and Laleh Bakhtiar. *The Risalah: Principles of Sufism*. [Chicago]: Great of the Islamic World, 2002. Print.

Jackson, Sherman A. *Islam and the Blackamerican: Looking toward the Third Resurrection*. Oxford: Oxford UP, 2005. Print.
Karim, Al-Haj Maulana Fazlul, Al-Hadis (Mishkat-ul-Masabih. Islamic Book Service 1989

King Jr., Martin Luther, Why We Can't Wait. Signet Classic, 2000

Levering Lewis, David. W.E.B. DuBois, The Fight for Equality and The American Century, 1919 – 1963. H.B. Fenn and Company Ltd., 2000

Latif, Syed Abdul Dr., The Mind Al-Qur'an Builds. Kazi Publication, 1983Maududi, S. Abul A'La, A Short History of the Revivalist Movement in Islam. Islamic Publications Limited, 1992

Mervyn Hiskett, The Sword of Truth, The Life and Times of the Sheu Ususman dan Fodio, Northwestern University Press, 1994

Mumisa, Michael, Islamic Law, Theory and Interpretation. Amana Publications, 2002

Nyang, Sulayman S., Islam in the United States of America. Kazi Publications, 1999

Nasr, Seyyed Hossein, The Heart of Islam, Enduring Values for Humanity. HarperCollins Publishers Inc., 2002

Omar, Abdul Mannan, Dictionary of The Holy Qur'an. Noor Foundation International Inc., 2006

Penrice, John, A Dictionary and Glossary of the Quran. Library of Islam, 1988

Robinson, Eugene, Disintegration, The Splintering of Black America. Random House, Inc., 2010

Saheeh International, Translation of the Meaning of the Qur'an, ABUL-QASIM PUBLISHING HOUSE, 1997, AL-MUNTADA AL-ISLAMI, 2004

Shah, Shahid, Alim, The World's Most Useful Islamic Software, Release 4. ISL Software Company, 1986-1996

Shuaibe, Faheem, A Message From A Grateful Student: The Final Lesson On Language And Logic From My Teacher Imam W. Deen Mohammed (Raa).

Siddiqi, Muhammad Iqbal, Ninety Nine Names of Allah. Kazi Publications, 1993

Woodson, Carter G., The Miseducation of The Negro. Africa World Press, Inc., 1990

Figure 1

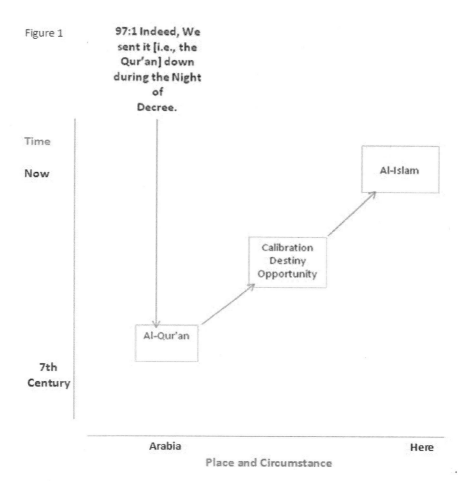

97:1 Indeed, We sent it [i.e., the Qur'an] down during the Night of Decree.

Time

Now

Al-Islam

Calibration
Destiny
Opportunity

Al-Qur'an

7th
Century

Arabia   Here

Place and Circumstance

Endnotes

---

[1] The root word of the Arabic word Dhikr is Dhakara (ذَكَرَ). The lexical root meaning is "to strike a man in the private parts". According to the Glossary of the Qur'an, Dhakara means; to commemorate, make mention of, bear in mind. Allah says in the Holy : 2:152. So remember Me; I will remember you. And be grateful to Me and do not deny Me. Among the many names for the Quran, Dhakara means; to commemorate, make mentio58. This is what We recite to you of the verses and the Wise Reminder [note: this ayah is an instance where I departed from the Saheeh International translation of the Qur'an]

[2] **3:19**. Indeed, the religion in the sight of Allah is Al-Islam. And those who were given the Scripture did not differ except after knowledge had come to them – out of jealous animosity between themselves. And whoever disbelieves in the verses of Allah, then indeed, Allah is swift in [taking] account.

إِنَّ الدِّينَ عِندَ اللَّهِ الْإِسْلَامُ ۗ وَمَا اخْتَلَفَ الَّذِينَ أُوتُوا الْكِتَابَ إِلَّا مِنْ بَعْدِ مَا جَاءَهُمُ الْعِلْمُ بَغْيًا بَيْنَهُمْ ۗ وَمَنْ يَكْفُرْ بِآيَاتِ اللَّهِ فَإِنَّ اللَّهَ سَرِيعُ الْحِسَابِ

[3] I prefer "Black" as opposed to African-American, although I do use the terms interchangeably. I think the term African-American is too broad. I also use a capital "B" in Black. Black people had to conduct a campaign to gain acceptance of a capital "N" in Negro, so it makes no sense to me to use a lower case 'B" in Black as both terms, including African-American refer to the same people. In an infamous footnote in WEB DuBois groundbreaking 1899 study, the Philadelphia Negro, Du Bois wrote, I shall throughout this study use the term "Negro," to designate all persons of Negro descent, although the appellation is to some extent illogical. I shall, moreover, capitalize the word, because I believe that eight million Americans are entitled to a capital letter". On this point, Booker T. Washington and DuBois, who's disagreement on the tactics to solve Negro problems are legendary agreed. Professor Booker T. Washington, being politely interrogated ... as to whether negroes ought to be called 'negroes' or 'members of the colored race' has replied that it has long been his own practice to write and speak of members of his race as negroes, and when using the term 'negro' as a race designation to employ the capital 'N' ["Harper's Weekly," June 2, 1906] ref:

http://www.etymonline.com/index.php?term=negro, 4/14/12. However, if I quote a source that does not capitalize the 'B" in Black, I do not change the quote.

[4] Allah, the proper name applied to the Being who exists necessarily, by Himself, comprising all the attributes of perfection.

[5] The Future of the Race, Henry Louis Gates, Jr. and Cornel West, p. 79 - 80

[6] I have extended Dr. West's observation about DuBois' spiritual strivings and often use used DuBois' life struggle (jihad) and analysis as the baseline for my effort to reconcile Islam as expressed in the Qur'an and Sunnah with the Black experience as I believe that that formative years of the Black American Muslim experience developed during the 20th century and is foremost in terms of time and scholarship during this period. As noted by David Levering in W.E.B, DuBois, The Fight For Equality and the American Century, 1919 – 1963, "To know DuBois was to become acquainted with the problem of the twentieth century – the problem of the color line – in one of the most intensely complex embodiments, and the experience of knowing Dubois was frequently a searing one. The author of the Souls of Black Folk comported himself as the avatar of a race whose troubled fate he was predestined to interpret and to direct". (p.2) He also wrote "In the course of his long, turbulent career, W. E. B. Du Bois attempted virtually every possible solution to the problem of twentieth-century racism—scholarship, propaganda, integration, national self-determination, human rights, cultural and economic separatism, , politics, international communism, expatriation, third world solidarity." (p. 571) DuBois himself stated in Dusk of Dawn, "Thus evidently to me and to others I did little to create my day or greatly change it; but I did exemplify it and thus for all time my life is significant for all lives of men."(p. 4)

[7] In The Study of the Negro Problems[1898] , DuBois stated, Now first we should study the Negro problems in order to distinguish between the different and distinct problems affecting this race. Nothing makes intelligent discussion of the Negro's position so fruitless as the repeated failure to discriminate between the different questions that concern him. If a Negro discusses the question, he is apt to discuss simply the problem of race prejudice; if a Southern white man writes on the subject he is apt to discuss problems of ignorance, crime and social degradation; and yet each calls the problem he discusses the Negro problem, leaving in the dark background the really crucial question as to the relative importance of the many problems involved. Before we can begin to study the Negro intelligently, we must realize definitely that not only is he affected by all the varying social forces that act on any nation at

his stage of advancement, but that in addition to these there is reacting upon him the mighty power of a peculiar and unusual social environment which affects to some extent every other social force. http://www.webdubois.org/dbStudyofnprob.html

[8] Cornel West identified DuBois as the towering black scholar of the twentieth century (The Future of the Race, Henry Louis gates, Jr. (Cornel West p. 55) Henry Louis Gates offered up DuBois' name as Person of the twentieth Century to the editors of Time Magazine in response to a poll of various world leaders, ranking politicians, famous entertainers, leading intellectuals, and other such figures, soliciting their nominations. (DuBois on Religion, Edited by Phil Zukerman, p. 1)

[9] I am using this metaphorically. **The Souls of Black Folk** is a classic work of American literature by W. E. B. Du Bois. It is a seminal work in the history of sociology, and a cornerstone of African-American literary history, http://en.wikipedia.org/wiki/The_Souls_of_Black_Folk, 9/5/11

[10] I am referring primarily to the Nation of Islam and the Moorish Science Temple. Edward E. Curtis IV argues in his book, Islam in Black America, p. 6, "The essential point is that any tradition, whether religious or not, is fashioned by human beings, who operate in historical time. "What people of faith share," Wilfred Cantwell Smith argued, "is not necessarily common definitions of what their religion means, but a common history." Hence, no person should be understood simply as a product of his or her tradition, but rather as a participant in that tradition. Faith is not "generated and sustained and shaped" by a religious tradition, according to Smith; rather, a person's faith is the result of his or her participation in "one historical phase" of an ongoing process. Moreover, these processes cannot be "reified" or "precisely delimited."[13] To take this reasoning to its logical conclusion, I would argue that the student of Islam should not even insist on using a person's identification with the Qur'an as a kind of minimal definition of what it means to be a Muslim. Instead, wherever and whenever a person calls himself or herself Muslim, scholars should include this person's voice in their understanding of what constitutes Islam. The mere fact that one has labeled oneself a Muslim indicates some sort of participation, however slight, in the process of Islamic history. That participation, in my view, is worthy of both scholarly attention, and in Hodgson's words, "human respect and recognition."

[11] Sherman Jackson argues in Islam and The Blackamerican, Looking Toward The Third resurrection that Blackamerican "Islamizers" like the Honorable Elijah Muhammad, founder of the Nation of Islam and Noble Drew Ali, founder of the Moorish Science Temple were able to co-opt, legitimize and even popularize the religion among the Blackamerican masses. p. 29

[12] A Short History of the Revivalist Movement in Islam, S. Abul A'La Maududi, p. 34

[13] One of Allah's names is Al-Khalaq, The Creator

[14] 47:24 Then do they not reflect upon the Qur'an, or are there locks upon [their] hearts?

[15] **10:100** And it is not for a soul [i.e., anyone] to believe except by permission of Allah, and He will place defilement upon those who will not use reason.

[16] **53:39** And that there is not for man except that [good] for which he strives

[17] One of Allah's names is Ar-Rabb, The Lord

[18] http://en.wikipedia.org/wiki/Serenity_Prayer, 8/19/12

[19] It should be noted that I was raised to be a Christian, but chose Al-Islam as I began my spiritual quest. I will explain my acceptance of Al-Islam in a later work; Insha Allah.

[20] Dictionary of the Holy Qur'an, Abdul Mannan Omar, p. 19-D

[21] Islam in Focus, Hammudah 'Abd al 'Ati, p.7

[22] 45:18. Then We put you, [O Muhammad], on an ordained way [Sharia] concerning the matter [of religion]; so follow it and do not follow the inclinations of those who do not know.

[23] http://www.saylor.org/site/wp-content/uploads/2011/08/HIST351-2.3.2-Sharia.pdf, 2/20/12

[24] W.E.B. DuBois on Race and Culture, page 93

[25] PBUH is an abbreviation for 'Peace Be Upon Him"

[26] A fairly common historical refrain of Civil Rights workers and activists including abolitionists was has been the complete bifurcation of America's expressed egalitarian and Christian values and its treatment of Blacks, woman and other people of color. DuBois stated, "A nation's religion is its life, and as such white Christianity is a miserable failure." (Darkwater, 1919, p. 21) In the Souls of Black Folks, DuBois confirmed the values of the Strivings of Negro People are rooted in American values by stating, "By every civilized and peaceful method we must strive for the rights which the world accords to men, clinging unwaveringly to those great words which the sons of the Fathers would fain forget: "We hold these truths to be self-evident: That all men are created equal; that they are endowed by their Creator with certain unalienable rights; that among these are life, liberty, and the pursuit of happiness." (Souls of Black Folks, p. 47)

[27] 14:4 And We did not send any messenger except [speaking] in the language of his people to state clearly for them, and Allah sends astray [thereby] whom He wills and guides whom He wills. And He is the Exalted in Might, the Wise.

[28] I think one of the advantages of the Black Muslim community is that we are young enough in Al-Islam that we can still tell the difference between religion, culture and personal history whereas some Muslims that use traditional many Muslims that accept a "traditional" understanding of Al-Islam consciously or unconsciously lump all of these influences into a big box called "Islam". I believe Black American Muslims, along with the children of immigrants from Muslim countries are strategically positioned to do the onion peeling that will be required to develop an Al-Islam that is appropriate for this time, place and circumstance and to live up to Allah's revelation:

> 5:54 O you who have believed, whoever of you should revert from his religion – Allah will bring forth [in place of them] a people He will love and who will love Him [who are] humble toward the believers, powerful against the disbelievers; they strive in the cause of Allah and do not fear the blame of a critic. That is the favor of Allah; He bestows it upon whom He wills. And Allah is all-Encompassing and Knowing.

[29] 41:40. Indeed, those who inject deviation into Our verses are not concealed from Us. So, is he who is cast into the Fire better or he who comes secure on the Day of Resurrection? Do whatever you will; indeed, He is Seeing of what you do.

[30] The Arabic word Ayatun (آية) is often translated "verse" in English and means A sign, miracle, a name given to the verses of the Qur'an, each of which is held to be a miracle. (Glossary of the Qur'an)

[31] The Arabic word Sunnah means a law, ordinance, line of conduct, mode of life, punishment

[32] **57:27** Then We sent following their footsteps [i.e., traditions] Our messengers and followed [them] with Jesus, the son of Mary, and gave him the Gospel. And We placed in the hearts of those who followed him compassion and mercy **and monasticism, which they innovated; We did not prescribe it for them except [that they did so] seeking the approval of Allah**. But they did not observe it with due observance. So We gave the ones who believed among them their reward, but many of them are defiantly disobedient.

[33] Sahih Al-Bukhari Hadith
Hadith 7.1   Narrated by
Anas bin Malik

A group of three men came to the houses of the wives of the Prophet asking how the Prophet worshipped (Allah), and when they were informed about that, they considered their worship insufficient and said, "Where are we from the Prophet as his past and future sins have been forgiven." Then one of them said, "I will offer the prayer throughout the night forever." The other said, "I will fast throughout the year and will not break my fast." The third said, "I will keep away from the women and will not marry forever." Allah's Apostle came to them and said, "Are you the same people who said so-and-so? By Allah, I am more submissive to Allah and more afraid of Him than you; yet I fast and break my fast, I do sleep and I also marry women. So he who does not follow my tradition in religion, is not from me (not one of my followers)."

[34] 25:63. And the servants of the Most Gracious are those who walk upon the earth easily, and when the ignorant address them [harshly], they say [words of] peace,
25:64. And those who spend [part of] the night to their Lord prostrating and standing [in prayer]
25:65. And those who say, "Our Lord, avert from us the punishment of Hell. Indeed, its punishment is ever adhering;
25:66. Indeed, it is evil as a settlement and residence."
25:67. And [they are] those who, when they spend, do so not excessively or sparingly but are ever, between that, [justly] moderate
25:68. And those who do not invoke with Allah another deity or kill the soul which Allah has forbidden [to be killed], except by right, and do not commit unlawful sexual intercourse. And whoever should do that will meet a penalty.

25:69. Multiplied for him is the punishment on the Day of Resurrection, and he will abide therein humiliated –

25:70. Except for those who repent, believe and do righteous work. For them Allah will replace their evil deeds with good. And ever is Allah Forgiving and Merciful.

25:71. And he who repents and does righteousness does indeed turn to Allah with [accepted] repentance.

25:72. And [they are] those who do not testify to falsehood, and when they pass near ill speech, they pass by with dignity.

25:73. And those who, when reminded of the verses of their Lord, do not fall upon them deaf and blind.

25:74. And those who say, "Our Lord, grant us from among our wives and offspring comfort to our eyes and make us a leader [i.e., example] for the righteous."

[35] Sahih Al-Bukhari Hadith, **Hadith 3.733**   Narrated by **Abdullah bin Umar**

The last line of this hadith actually includes the following line text:

." I definitely heard the above from the Prophet and think that the Prophet also said, "A man is a guardian of his father's property and responsible for his charges; so everyone of you is a guardian and responsible for his charges."

[36] A Study of Spirituality in the Workplace In The Washington, DC Metropolitan Area, Dawud Abdur-Rahman, p. 2

[37] **22:36** And the camels and cattle We have appointed for you as among the symbols [i.e., rites] of Allah; for you therein is good. So mention the name of Allah upon them when lined up [for sacrifice]; and when they are [lifeless] on their sides, then eat from them and feed the needy [who does not seek aid] and the beggar. Thus have We subjected them to you that you may be grateful.

22:37 Their meat will not reach Allah, nor will their blood, but what reaches Him is piety from you. Thus have We subjected them to you that you may glorify Allah for that [to] which He has guided you; and give good tidings to the doers of good.

[38] Sahih Muslim Hadith
Hadith 1   Narrated by
Narrated by
Abdullah ibn Umar ibn al-Khattab

It is narrated on the authority of Yahya ibn Ya'mar that the first man who discussed Qadr (Divine Decree) in Basrah was Ma'bad al-Juhani. Humayd ibn AbdurRahman al-Himyari and I set out for Pilgrimage or for Umrah and said: Should it so happen that we come into contact with one of the Companions of the Messenger of Allah (peace be upon him) we shall ask him about what is talked about Taqdir (Division Decree). Accidentally we came across Abdullah ibn Umar ibn al-Khattab, while he was entering the mosque. My companion and I surrounded him. One of us (stood) on his right and the other stood on his left. I expected that my companion would authorize me to speak. I therefore said: AbuAbdurRahman! There have appeared some people in our land who recite the Holy Qur'an and pursue knowledge. And then after talking about their affairs, added: They (such people) claim that there is no such thing as Divine Decree and events are not predestined. He (Abdullah ibn Umar) said: When you happen to meet such people tell them that I have nothing to do with them and they have nothing to do with me. And verily they are in no way responsible for my (belief). Abdullah ibn Umar swore by Him (the Lord) (and said): If any one of them (who does not believe in the Divine Decree) had with him gold equal to the bulk of (the mountain) Uhud and then, it (in the way of Allah), Allah would not accept it unless he affirmed his faith in Divine Decree. He further said: My father, Umar ibn al-Khattab, told me: One day we were sitting in the company of Allah's Apostle (peace be upon him) when there appeared before us a man dressed in pure white clothes, his hair extraordinarily black. There were no signs of travel on him. None amongst us recognized him. At last he sat with the Apostle (peace be upon him) He knelt before him placed his palms on his thighs and said: Muhammad, inform me about al-Islam. The Messenger of Allah (peace be upon him) said: Al-Islam implies that you testify that there is no god but Allah and that Muhammad is the messenger of Allah, and you establish prayer, pay Zakat, observe the fast of Ramadan, and perform pilgrimage to the (House) if you are solvent enough (to bear the expense of) the journey. He (the inquirer) said: You have told the truth. He (Umar ibn al-Khattab) said: It amazed us that he would put the question and then he would himself verify the truth. He (the inquirer) said: Inform me about Iman (faith). He (the Holy Prophet) replied: That you affirm your faith in Allah, in His angels, in His Books, in His Apostles, in the Day of Judgment, and you affirm your faith in the Divine Decree about good and evil. He (the inquirer) said: You have told the truth. He (the inquirer) again said: **Inform me about al-Ihsan (performance of good deeds). He (the Holy Prophet) said: That you worship Allah as if you are seeing Him, for though you don't see Him, He, verily, sees you.** He (the enquirer) again said: Inform me about the hour (of the Doom). He (the Holy Prophet) remarked: One who is asked knows no more than the one who is inquiring (about it). He (the inquirer) said: Tell me some of its indications. He (the Holy Prophet) said:

That the slave-girl will give birth to her mistress and master, that you will find barefooted, destitute goat-herds vying with one another in the construction of magnificent buildings. He (the narrator, Umar ibn al-Khattab) said: Then he (the inquirer) went on his way but I stayed with him (the Holy Prophet) for a long while. He then, said to me: Umar, do you know who this inquirer was? I replied: Allah and His Apostle knows best. He (the Holy Prophet) remarked: He was Gabriel (the angel). He came to you in order to instruct you in matters of religion.

[39] Ibadat (عبادت): Obedience; Worship; Piety; The impress of Divine attributes and imbibing and reflecting them on one's own person; Complete and utmost humility; submissiveness; Service the idea of 'Ibadat in the Qur'an lies not in a mere declaration of glory of God by lips and performance of certain rites or service, e.g., Prayer, Fasting etc…, but it is in fact the imbibing of Divine morals and receiving their impress and imbibing his ways and complete obedience to Him. Dictionary of the Holy Qur'an, p. 355

[40] An Arabic English Lexicon by Edward William Lane Part 1, p. 83

[41] This is a slightly modified quote taken from Tawhid: Its Relevance For thought and Life, Isma'il Raji Faruqi, p. 1.

[42] **22:78** And strive for Allah with the striving due to Him. He has chosen you and has not placed upon you in the religion any difficulty. [It is] the religion of your father, Abraham. He [i.e., Allah] named you "Muslims" before [in former scriptures] and in this [revelation] that the Messenger may be a witness over you and you may be witnesses over the people. So establish prayer and give zakah and hold fast to Allah. He is your protector; and excellent is the protector, and excellent is the helper.

[43] 30:20 And of His signs is that He created you from dust; then, suddenly you were human beings dispersing [throughout the earth].

45: 3. Indeed, within the heavens and earth are signs for the believers. 45:4. And in the creation of yourselves and what He disperses of moving creatures are signs for people who are certain [in faith].

[44] **5:35** O you who have believed, fear Allah and seek the means [of nearness] to Him and strive in His cause that you may succeed.
17:57 Those whom they invoke seek means of access to their Lord, [striving as to] which of them would be nearest, and they hope for His mercy and fear His punishment. Indeed, the punishment of your Lord is ever feared.

[45] **Shia Islam** (Arabic: شيعة, Shīʿah) is the second largest <u>denomination</u> of <u>Islam</u>. Adherents of Shia Islam are called **Shi'is** [ˈshē-ēz], **Shi'ites**, or **Shias**. "Shia" is the short form of the historic phrase Shīʿatu ʿAlī (شيعة علي), meaning "followers of <u>Ali</u>", "faction of Ali", or "party of Ali". [1][2][3][4][5].
http://en.wikipedia.org/wiki/Shia_Islam, 4/29/12

[46] **Ayatollah** (<u>Persian</u>: آيت‌الله āyatollāh from <u>Arabic</u>: آية الله, āyatu l-Lāh "Sign of God"; UK: /aɪəˈtɒlə/, US: /aɪətoʊlə/) is a high ranking title given to <u>Usuli Twelver</u> <u>Shīʿah</u> clerics. Those who carry the title are <u>experts</u> in <u>Islamic studies</u> such as <u>jurisprudence</u>, <u>ethics</u>, and <u>philosophy</u> and usually teach in <u>Islamic seminaries</u>. http://en.wikipedia.org/wiki/Ayatollah, 11/12/11

[47] 51: 20 And on the earth are signs for the certain [in faith]
51:21 And in yourselves. Then will you not see?

[48] This hadith is generally accepted to be weak, but is accepted by some scholars. http://friendsofdeoband.wordpress.com/2012/09/14/analysis-of-hadith-the-greater-jihad/

[49] 50:16. And We have already created man and know what his soul whispers to him, and We are closer   to him than [his] jugular vein

[50] DuBois' definition of Double Consciousness was, "It is a peculiar sensation, this double-consciousness, this sense of always looking at one's self through the eyes of others, of measuring one's soul by the tape of a world that looks on in amused contempt and pity. One ever feels his twoness,—an American, a Negro; two souls, two thoughts, two unreconciled strivings; two warring ideals in one dark body, whose dogged strength alone keeps it from being torn asunder., Souls of Black Folks, p. 9

[51] **2:39**   And those who disbelieve and deny Our signs – those will be companions of the Fire; they will abide therein eternally.

[52] A Dictionary and Glossary of the Qur'an, John Penrice, p. 71

[53] Even in the 'Black" a single label not necessarily applicable. During the past four decades, Eugene Robinson, in Disintegration, The Splintering of Black America, outlines framework for discussing the four subgroups that now are collectively grouped in "Black" or "African-American" America; the Abandoned, a large and growing underclass concentrated in the inner cities and depressed pockets of the rural South; the Transcendent elite with such enormous wealth, power, and influence that even "white folks have to genuflect" and; an Emergent community made up of mixed-race families and black immigrants from Africa and the Caribbean.

[54] Washington Post columnist Eugene Robinson authored an interesting book titled, Disintegration, The Splintering of Black America, that advocates the perspective that since the Civil Rights Movement, even the Black American Community is more distinctly diverse and can be categorized into four groups:

- A Mainstream middle-class majority with a full ownership stake in American society;
- A large, Abandoned minority with less hope of escaping poverty and dysfunction than at any time since Reconstruction's crushing end;
- A small Transcendent elite with such enormous wealth, power, and influence that even white folks have to genuflect;
- Two newly Emergent groups – individuals of mixed-race heritage and communities of recent black immigrants – that make us wonder what "black" is even supposed to mean.

•

[55] Black Pilgrimage to Islam, Robert Dannin, p. 82

[56] Sahih Al-Bukhari Hadith
Hadith 4.593   Narrated by
Abu Huraira

Some people asked the Prophet: "Who is the most honorable amongst the people?" He replied, "The most honorable among them is the one who is the most Allah-fearing." They said, "O Allah's Prophet! We do not ask about this." He said, "Then the most honorable person is Joseph, Allah's Prophet, the son of Allah's Prophet, the son of Allah's Prophet, the son of Allah's Khalil." They said, "We do not ask about this." He said, "Then you want to ask me about the Arabs' descent?" They said, "Yes." He said, "Those who were best in the pre-Islamic period, are the best in Islam, if they comprehend (the religious knowledge)."

[57] Dr. Sherman Jackson in Islam and The Black American, Looking Toward the Third Resurrection, defines the "Third Resurrection" as follows: "The challenge, as such , for Blackamerican Muslims has become how to negotiate a dignified, black, American existence without flouting the legitimate aspects of the agenda of Black Religion or vesting the latter with too much authority, and without falling victim to the ideological claims, prejudices, and false obsessions of immigrant Islam.

This book will argue that the answer to this challenge lies in the Blackamerican Muslim mastery and appropriation of the Sunni super-tradition, a development that I refer to as the 'Third Resurrection." In this new relationship however, mastery and appropriation are critical to success."

---

[58] Islam in Black America, Identity, Liberation and Difference in African-American Thought, Edward E. Curtis IV, p. 5

[59] The revelation of the Qur'an and the Prophethood of Muhammad Ibn Abdullah (PBUH) revived the pure monotheism established by Prophet Abraham:

3:67. Abraham was neither a Jew nor a Christian, but he was one inclining toward truth, a Muslim [submitting to Allah]. And he was not of the polytheists.
3:68. Indeed, the most worthy of Abraham among the people are those who followed him [in submission to Allah] and this prophet [i.e., Muhammad] and those who believe [in his message]. And Allah is the ally of the believers.

[60] The meaning of the Arabic word Deen (دين) means Custom, institution, religion, the true faith, obedience, judgment. The root word means to be indebted, to judge (A Dictionary and Glossary of the Qur'an, p. 50)

[61] 5:48. And We have revealed to you, [O Muhammad], the Book [i.e., the Qur'an] in truth, confirming that which preceded it of the Scripture and as a criterion over it. So judge between them by what Allah has revealed and do not follow their inclinations away from what has come to you of the truth. **To each of you We prescribed a law and a method.** Had Allah willed, He would have made you one nation [united in religion], but [He intended] to test you in what He has given you; so race to [all that is] good. To Allah is your return all together, and He will [then] inform you concerning that over which you used to differ.

[62] Seerah is the Arabic word for "biography"

[63] **25:52** So do not obey the disbelievers, and strive against them with it [i.e., the Qur'an] a great striving.

[64] Al-Hadis, an English Translation and Commentary of Miskat-ul-Masabih, within Arabic Text, Alhaj Maulana Fazlu Karim, vol 3, p. 589

[65] It should be noted that some translations of this hadith include a reference to the Prophet leaving his Sunnah while at the same time this reference does not appear all recording of this hadith in the original Arabic. Also, there are other versions of this hadith, some that indicate the Propjet said he left the Quran and Sunnah as well as hadith that indicate the Prophet left the Qur'an and his Household.

[66] 2:2. This is the Book about which there is no doubt, a guidance for those conscious of Allah

[67] **7:157** Those who follow the Messenger, the unlettered prophet, whom they find written [i.e., mentioned] in what they have of the Torah and the Gospel, who enjoins upon them what is right and forbids them what is wrong and makes lawful for them the good things and prohibits for them the evil and relieves them of their burden and the shackles which were upon them. So they who have believed in him, honored him, supported him and followed the light which was sent down with him – it is those who will be the successful.

[68] 54: 4 And there has already come to them of information that in which there is deterrence –
54:5 Extensive wisdom – but warning does not avail [them].

[69] 25:1 Blessed is He who sent down the Criterion upon His Servant that he may be to the worlds a warner –

[70] 81:25. And it [i.e., the Qur'an] is not the word of a devil, expelled [from the heavens].
81:26. So where are you going?
81:27. It is not except a reminder to the worlds
81:28. For whoever wills among you to take a right course.
81:29. And you do not will except that Allah wills – Lord of the worlds.

[71] **3:137** Similar situations [as yours] have passed on before you, so proceed throughout the earth and observe how was the end of those who denied.

[72] 20:44. And speak to him with gentle speech that perhaps he may be reminded or fear [Allah]."

[73] A Sufi is one that practices Sufism. **Sufism or taṣawwuf** (Arabic: تصوّف) is defined by its adherents as the inner, mystical dimension of Islam, http://en.wikipedia.org/wiki/Sufism, 4/29/12

[74] The Risalah, Principles of Sufism, Abu-l- Qasim 'Abd-al-Karim bin Hawazin al-Qushayri, p. 435

[75] The Mis-Education of The Negro, Carter G. Woodson, p. xiii

[76] 5:54. O you who have believed, whoever of you should revert from his religion —4. O you who have believed, whoever of you should revert from his religion, love Him [who are] humble toward the believers, powerful against the disbelievers; they strive in the cause of Allah and do not fear the blame of a critic. That is the favor of Allah; He bestows it upon whom He wills. And Allah is all-Encompassing and Knowing.

[77] The Sword of Truth, The Life and Times of the Shehu Ususman dan Fodio, Mervyn Hiskett, p. 5, 6
[78] Black Religion and Black Radicalism, An Interpretation of the Religious History of African Americans, Gayraud S. Wilmore, p. 15

[79] **2:170**. And when it is said to them, "Follow what Allah has revealed," they say, "Rather, we will follow that which we found our fathers doing." Even though their fathers understood nothing, nor were they guided?

[80] **Warith Deen Mohammed** (born **Wallace D. Muhammad**; October 30, 1933 – September 9, 2008) also known as W. Deen Mohammed or Imam W. Deen Muhammad, was a progressive African American Muslim leader, theologian, philosopher, Muslim revivalist and Islamic thinker (1975 to 2008) who disbanded the original Nation of Islam in 1976 and transformed it into an orthodox mainstream Islamic movement, the World Community of Al-Islam in the West which later became the American Society of Muslims. He was a son of Elijah Muhammad, the leader of the Nation of Islam from 1933 to 1975., http://en.wikipedia.org/wiki/Warith_Deen_Mohammed, 2/19/12

[81] Dr. Sherman Jackson acknowledged this publically in a piece entitled, Imam W. D. Mohammed and The Third Resurrection by Dr. Sherman Jackson , upon his death: http://www.marcmanley.com/imam-w-d-mohammed-and-the-third-resurrection-by-dr-sherman-jackson/, 5/29/11 Unifying efforts like this in the process to move forward with common cause along the path of Al-Islam.

[82] Islam in Black America, Identity, Liberation and Difference in African-American Islamic Thought, Edward E. Curtis IV, P. 127

[83] A Message From A Grateful Student: The Final Lesson On Language And Logic From My Teacher Imam W. Deen Mohammed, p. 29, Imam Faheem Shuaibe

[84] A Message From A Grateful Student: The Final Lesson On Language And Logic From My Teacher Imam W. Deen Mohammed, p. 5, Imam Faheem Shuaibe

---

[85] 5:54. O you who have believed, whoever of you should revert from his religion –:54. O you who have believed, whoever of you should revert from his religion love Him [who are] humble toward the believers, powerful against the disbelievers; they strive in the cause of Allah and do not fear the blame of a critic. That is the favor of Allah; He bestows it upon whom He wills. And Allah is all-Encompassing and Knowing.

[86] 4:139. Those who take disbelievers as allies instead of the believers. Do they seek with them honor [through power]? But indeed, honor belongs to Allah entirely.

[87] Newsweek, 9/5/05, <u>A New Welcoming Spirit in the Mosque</u> ; "Children of immigrants are the fastest growing group among the nation's estimated 7 million Muslims, and they're changing the face of Islam in this country by combining their faith with the American tradition of diversity. In Orange County [California], youth-group members have similar stories; their strong ties with Islam really started in college, when the bonded with a mixed group of Muslims. **This scenario was unthinkable even 15 years ago for immigrants who stuck with their own for support and for African-American Muslims who were still working through the racial exclusivity of the Nation of Islam.** Those divisions mean little to the twenty somethings in Orange County." "It's all about Muslim identity now, " says Haider Javed, 25, the center's youth coordinator. He wears jeans and a skullcap and seems to know everyone in the giant building. "You're searching for yourself," Javed says. I'm not an American kid who goes out and drinks. I'm not entirely Pakistani either. But I am thoroughly Muslim. I feel comfortable at the Islamic Center, like this is where I Actually belong.", p. 52

[88] Sahih Al-Bukhari Hadith, **Hadith 6.544** Narrated by **Abu Huraira**

[89] Qadr, (قدر): That which is determined, or predestined of God, measure, value, power (A Dictionary and Glossary of the Qur'an, p. 115)

[90] Al-Tirmidhi Hadith
Hadith 98   Narrated by
AbuHurayrah

Allah's Messenger (peace be upon him) came to us as we had been arguing with each other about the Divine Decree (al-Qadr). He was so annoyed that his face became as red as if there had been squeezed on his cheeks the flesh of pomegranates. He said: Is this what you have been commanded to do, is this with which I have been sent to you?

Those who had gone before you were destroyed as they disputed about it. I adjure you, I adjure you not to fall into argumentation in regard to it. Tirmidhi transmitted it. Ibn Majah transmitted something similar from Abdullah ibn Amr ibn al-'As in Kitab al-Qadr No. 0085.

[91] 5: 35. O you who have believed, fear Allah and seek the means [of nearness] to Him and strive in His cause that you may succeed.

[92] Sahih Al-Bukhari Hadith
Hadith 3.706   Narrated by
Umar bin Al Khattab

The Prophet said, "The (reward of) deeds depend on intentions, and every person will get the reward according to what he intends. So, whoever migrated for Allah and His Apostle, then his migration will be for Allah and His Apostle, and whoever migrated for worldly benefits or for marrying a woman, then his migration will be for what he migrated for." (See Hadith No. 1, Vol. 1)

[93] Dictionary and Glossary of the Qur'an

[94] 29:69. And those who strive for Us – We will surely guide them to Our ways. And indeed, Allah is with the doers of good.

[95] 49:14. The Bedouins say, "We have believed." Say, "You have not [yet] believed; but say [instead], 'We have submitted,' for faith has not yet entered your hearts. And if you obey Allah and His Messenger, He will not deprive you from your deeds of anything. Indeed, Allah is Forgiving and Merciful."

[96] Al-Tirmidhi Hadith
Hadith 121   Narrated by
Abdullah ibn Abbas

Allah's Apostle (peace be upon him) said: Allah made covenant (with the whole of mankind) while creating it from Adam's back in Na'man i.e. Arafah and emitting from his loins all his offspring that He created and scattering them before Him like ant. He then spoke to them in their presence and said: `Am I not your Lord? They answered: Yes, we do bear witness thereto (of this We remind you) lest you say on the Day of Resurrection: Verily, we were unaware of this. Or lest you say: Verily, these were our forefathers in times gone by, who began to ascribe divinity to other things besides Allah and we were but their late offspring. Wilt Thou then destroy us for doings of those inventors of falsehood.' (7:172-173)

[97] This is one of few instances where deviated from the Saheeh International Qur'an translation, I used the translation from Ibn Kathir.

Full Context:

13:10 It is the same (to Him) whether any of you conceals his speech or declares it openly, whether he be hid by night or goes forth freely by day. 13:11 For him (each person), there are angels in succession, before and behind him. They guard him by the command of Allah. Verily, Allah will not change the (good) condition of a people as long as they do not change their state (of goodness) themselves. But when Allah wills a people's punishment, there can be no turning it back, and they will find besides Him no protector.)

[98] The Future of the Race, Henry Louis Gates, Jr. and Cornel West, p. 79 - 80

[99] A Dictionary and Glossary of the Quran, John Penrice, p. 30

[100] 9:112. [Such believers are] the repentant, the worshippers, the praisers [of Allah], the travelers [for His cause], those who bow and prostrate [in prayer], those who enjoin what is right and forbid what is wrong, and those who observe the limits [set by] Allah. And give good tidings to the believers.

[101] Dictionary of the Holy Qur'an, Abdul Mannan Omar, p. 106

[102] http://www.blackpast.org/?q=1857-frederick-douglass-if-there-no-struggle-there-no-progress, 10/6/12

[103] Sunan of Abu-Dawood
Hadith 5100 Narrated by
Wathilah ibn al-Asqa'

I asked: Apostle of Allah! what is party spirit? He replied: That you should help your people in wrongdoing.

[104] **22:40** [They are] those who have been evicted from their homes without right – only because they say, "Our Lord is Allah." And were it not that Allah checks the people, some by means of others, there would have been demolished monasteries, churches, synagogues, and mosques in which the name of Allah is much mentioned [i.e., praised]. And Allah will surely support those who support Him [i.e., His cause]. Indeed, Allah is Powerful and Exalted in Might.

[105] 67:3. [And] who created seven heavens in layers. You do not see in the creation of the Most Merciful any inconsistency. So return [your] vision [to the sky]; do you see any breaks?
67:4. Then return [your] vision twice again. [Your] vision will return to you humbled while it is fatigued.

[106] I intend to detail my views on Christianity in a later work, Insha Allah (Allah willing)
[107] Some Christians believe that by accepting the Crucifixion and Resurrection of Jesus (PBUH), the promise of salvation to the Jews moves to or is shared with Christians.

[108] Sahih Muslim Hadith, **Hadith 6653** Narrated by **AbuHurayrah**

[109] http://en.wikipedia.org/wiki/The_Farewell_Sermon, 4/16/11

[110] Qadr is means Allah's Power

[111] In critical race theory, **white privilege** is a way of conceptualizing racial inequalities that focuses as much on the advantages that white people accrue from society as on the disadvantages that people of color experience., http://en.wikipedia.org/wiki/White_privilege, 2/13/12

[112] Souls of Black Folk, W.E.B. DuBois, p. 12

[113] The Arabic word Iqra means to read and recite. The Prophet Muhammad recited the Qur'an as it was revealed by Allah through the Angel Gabriel (Jabril). It was written down by his companions.

96:1 Recite in the name of your Lord who created –
96:2 Created man from a clinging substance.
96:3 Recite, and your Lord is the most Generous –
96:4 Who taught by the pen –
96:5 Taught man that which he knew not.

[114] http://www.brainyquote.com/quotes/authors/h/harriet_tubman.html, 7/7/11

[115] W.E.B. DuBois on Race and Culture, edited by Bell, Grosholz, Stewart, p. 263

---

[116] DuBois, Development of a People, 1904: In other words, if we are to judge intelligently or clearly of the development of a people, we must allow ourselves neither to be dazzled by figures nor misled by inapt comparisons, but we must seek to know what human advancement historically considered has meant and what it means to-day, and from such criteria we may then judge the condition, development and needs of the group before us. I want then to mention briefly the steps which groups of men have usually taken in their forward struggling, and to ask which of these steps the Negroes of the United States have taken and how far they have gone. In such comparisons we cannot, unfortunately, have the aid of exact statistics, for actual measurement of social phenomena is peculiar to the Nineteenth century—that is, to an age when the culture Nations were full-grown, and we can only roughly indicate conditions in the days of their youth. A certain youth and childhood is common to all men in their mingled striving. Everywhere, glancing across the seas of human history, we note it. The average American community of to-day has grown by a slow, intricate and hesitating advance through four overlapping eras. First, there is the struggle for sheer physical existence—a struggle still waging among the submerged tenth, but settled for a majority of the community long years ago. Above this comes the accumulation for future subsistence—the saving and striving and transmuting of goods for use in days to come—a stage reached to-day tentatively for the middle classes and to an astounding degree by a few. Then in every community there goes on from the first, but with larger and larger emphasis as the years fly, some essay to train the young into the tradition of the fathers—their religion, thought and tricks of doing. And, finally, as the group meets other groups and comes into larger spiritual contact with nations, there is that transference and sifting and accumulation of the elements of human culture which makes for wider civilization and higher development. These four steps of subsistence, accumulation, education and culture-contact are not disconnected, discreet stages. No nation ever settles its problems of poverty and then turns to educating children; or first accumulates its wealth and then its culture. On the contrary, in every stage of a nation's growing all these efforts are present, and we designate any particular age of a people's development as (for instance) a struggle for existence, because, their conscious effort is more largely expended in this direction than in others; but despite this we all know, or ought to know, that no growing nation can spend its whole effort on to-day's food lest accumulation and training of children and learning of their neighbors—lest all these things so vitally necessary to advance be neglected, and the people, full-bellied though they be, stagnate and die because in one mighty struggle to live they forget the weightier objects of life.

[117] The Hadith are traditions of Muhammad, giving us important information about his life. They are usually narrations about a certain incident in which he said or did something. This is how Muslims determine the Sunnah (Muhammad's way of life.) It is key to Islam since Muslims are commanded to obey Muhammad and emulate him. In fact, four out of five of Islam's Pillars would not exist without the Hadith, therefore making Islam impossible to practice., http://wikiislam.net/wiki/Glossary_of_Islamic_Terms#H, 12-13-12

[118] "After the Egyptian and Indian, the Greek and Roman, the Teuton and Mongolian, the Negro is a sort of seventh son, born with a veil, and gifted with second-sight in this American world, —a world which yields him no true self-consciousness, but only lets him see himself through the revelation of the other world. It is a peculiar sensation, this double-consciousness, this sense of always looking at one's self through the eyes of others, of measuring one's soul by the tape of a world that looks on in amused contempt and pity. One ever feels his twoness,—an American, a Negro; two souls, two thoughts, two unreconciled strivings; two warring ideals in one dark body, whose dogged strength alone keeps it from being torn asunder.", Souls of Black Folk, W.E.B. DuBois, p. 8, 9

[119] 4: 175. So those who believe in Allah and hold fast to Him – He will admit them to mercy from Himself and bounty and guide them to Himself on a straight path.

[120] 21:106. Indeed, in this [Quran] is notification for a worshipping people.

[121] **33:21**   Ye have indeed in the Apostle of Allah a beautiful pattern of (conduct) for anyone whose hope is in Allah and the Final Day and who engages much in the praise of Allah.

68: 4. And indeed, you are of a great moral character.

[122] 45: 6. These are the verses of Allah which We recite to you in truth. Then in what statement after Allah and His verses will they believe?

[123] **4:1**. O mankind, fear your Lord, who created you from one soul and created from it its mate and dispersed from both of them many men and women. And fear Allah, through whom134 you ask one another,135 and the wombs.136 Indeed Allah is ever, over you, an Observer.

---

[124] Tasawwuf is a branch of Islamic knowledge which focuses on the spiritual development of the Muslim, http://www.tasawwuf.org/basics/what_tasawwuf.htm, 11/15/11.

The terms Sufism and Tasawuf are often used interchangeably

[125] Life in the family of origin (the family a person is born and raised in) is a tremendously powerful experience for everyone. And the impact of that experience is not restricted to childhood. The way we see ourselves, others, and the world is shaped in the setting of our family of origin. The views we develop there stay with us throughout life, Family Ties that Bind, A Self-Help Guide to Change through Family of Origin Therapy, Dr. Ronald W. Richardson, p. 1.

[126] **2:284**. To Allah belongs whatever is in the heavens and whatever is in the earth. Whether you show what is within yourselves or conceal it, Allah will bring you to account for it. Then He will forgive whom He wills and punish whom He wills, and Allah is over all things competent.

[127] 10: 99. And had your Lord willed, those on earth would have believed – all of them entirely. Then, [O Muhammad], would you compel the people in order that they become believers?

[128] 4: 36. Worship Allah and associate nothing with Him, and to parents do good, and to relatives, orphans, the needy, the near neighbor, the neighbor farther away, the companion at your side, the traveler, and those whom your right hands possess. Indeed,
Allah does not like those who are self-deluding and boastful,

[129] **3:133**. And hasten to forgiveness from your Lord and a garden [i.e., Paradise] as wide as the heavens and earth, prepared for the righteous **3:134**. Who spend [in the cause of Allah] during ease and hardship and who restrain anger and who pardon the people – and Allah loves the doers of good;

[130] **3:137** Similar situations [as yours] have passed on before you, so proceed throughout the earth and observe how was the end of those who denied.

[131] 22:78. And strive for Allah with the striving due to Him. He has chosen you and has not placed upon you in the religion any difficulty. [It is] the religion of your father, Abraham. He [i.e., Allah] named you "Muslims" before [in former scriptures] and in this [revelation] that the Messenger may be a witness over you and you may be witnesses over the people.

So establish prayer and give zakah and hold fast to Allah. He is your protector; and excellent is the protector, and excellent is the helper.

[132] An objective review of the Qur'an and Hadith illustrates that all the elements of the orientations to Al-Islam that ultimately became identified as Sunni Shia and Sufi and there.   It is just that some groups decided to have a particular orientation, focus and methodology to their practice of Al-Islam.

[133] **4:85**. Whoever intercedes for a good cause will have a share [i.e., reward] therefrom; and whoever intercedes for an evil cause will have a portion [i.e., burden] therefrom. And ever is Allah, over all things, a Keeper.

[134] 24:46. We have certainly sent down distinct verses. And Allah guides whom He wills to a straight path.

[135] **13:29** Those who have believed and done righteous deeds – a good state is theirs and a good return.

[136] The Mind Al-Qur'an Builds, Dr. Syed Abdul Latif, p. 125

[137] Wilmore, Gayraud S., Black Religion and Black Radicalism, An Interpretations of the Religious History of African Americans, p. 217

[138] Wilmore, Gayraud S., Black Religion and Black Radicalism, An Interpretations of the Religious History of African Americans, p. 217

[139] http://africanamericanquotes.org/booker-t.-washington.html, 7/7/11

[140] Come On People, On the Path From Victims to Victors, Bill Cosby, Alvin F. Poussaint, M.D., p. 40 - 41

[141] Islam and the Blackamerican, Looking Toward the Third Resurrection. P. 4

[142] Islam and the Blackamerican, Looking Toward the Third Resurrection. P. 73

[143] Islam in the United States of America, Sulayman S, Yang, p. 19

[144] To the point, although Malcolm changed his name to El Hajj Malik El Shabazz, he said he would continue to go by Malcolm X for as long as the situation that produced it exists.
http://www.youtube.com/watch?v=lx7RecMy2og&list=FLVNbfw-W4OaoxCtqqQLJl4A&index=4&feature=plpp_video

[145] http://www.brainyquote.com/quotes/authors/s/sojourner_truth.html, 1/16/12

[146] A Dictionary and Glossary of the Qur'an, p. 56

[147] The Heart of Islam, Enduring Values for Humanity, Sayyed Hossein Nasr, p. 204

[148] "What Is A 'Black Agenda", *Op-ed submission by Project 21,* http://afrospear.com/2010/03/19/what-is-a-black-agenda/, 5/31/11

[149] Sahih Al-Bukhari Hadith, **Hadith 2.480** Narrated by **Abu Huraira**

[150] Al-Tirmidhi Hadith
Hadith 179   Narrated by **AbuHurayrah**

Allah's Messenger (peace be upon him) said: (You are living) in an age that when he who abandons even one-tenth of that which he is prescribed, courts destruction. After this there will come a time when he who observes one-tenth of what is now prescribed will be saved. Transmitted by Tirmidhi.

[151] From the Souls of Black Folk, p. 14, "We the darker ones come even now not altogether
empty-handed: there are today no truer exponents of the pure human spirit of the Declaration of Independence than the American Negroes; there is no true American music but the wild sweet melodies of the Negro slave; the American fairy tales and folklore are Indian and African; and, all in all, we black men seem the sole oasis of simple faith and reverence in a dusty desert of dollars and smartness."

[152] The Conservation of Races, W.E.B. DuBois, p. 13

[153] The Strivings of the Negro People, W.E.B. DuBois, 1897

[154] **Tariq Ramadan** (Arabic: طارق رمضان; born 26 August 1962 in Geneva, Switzerland) is a Swiss academic and writer. He is also a Professor of Contemporary Islamic Studies in the Faculty of Oriental Studies at Oxford University. He advocates the study and re-interpretation of Islamic texts, and emphasizes the heterogeneous nature of Western Muslims, http://en.wikipedia.org/wiki/Tariq_Ramadan, 5/4/12

[155] The Future of Islam, John L. Esposito, p. 112

[156] Black Pilgrimage to Islam, Robert Danin, p. 254

[157] Wilmore, Gayraud S., Black Religion and Black Radicalism, An Interpretations of the Religious History of African Americans, p. 25

[158] Mumisa, Michael, Islamic Law Theory and Interpretation, p. 38

[159] The Qur'an and Woman, p. 80

[160] The Qur'an and Woman, Amina Wadud, p 101

[161] 81:8. And when the girl [who was] buried alive is asked
81:9. For what sin she was killed

[162] The World and Africa, An Inquiry into the part which Africa has played in World History, WEB DuBois, p. 207 - 208

[163] Statement by Professor Azizah Y. al-Hibri, Committee on Women's Rights and Gender Equality, European Parliament, April 17, 2008, http://www.europarl.europa.eu/document/activities/cont/200804/20080422 ATT27224/20080422ATT27224EN.pdf

[164] Statement by Professor Azizah Y. al-Hibri, Committee on Women's Rights and Gender Equality, European Parliament, April 17, 2008, http://www.europarl.europa.eu/document/activities/cont/200804/20080422 ATT27224/20080422ATT27224EN.pdf

[165] W.E.B. DuBois On Race and Culture, p. 128

[166] Alim, Islamic CD

[167] Islam and the Black American, Looking Toward the Third Resurrection, p. 51

[168] Sunan of Abu-Dawood
Hadith 2602   Narrated by
AbuSa'id al-Khudri

The Prophet (peace be upon him) said: When three are on a journey, they should appoint one of them as their commander.

[169] http://www.ohfp.org/

[170] The early Muslim community sought refuge in Abyssinia from persecution in Mecca. Cooperation with the Black church will be the key to any successful strategy that addresses relevant issues in the Black community.

[171] http://www.wjla.com/articles/2011/11/man-stabbed-killed-in-oxon-hill-69347.html, 4/24/12   Jakari's murderer was identified apprehended by police: http://www.washingtonpost.com/blogs/crime-scene/post/alexandria-man-arrested-in-oxon-hill-stabbing/2011/11/22/gIQA2CewlN_blog.html

[172] http://www.youtube.com/user/read1communications/featured

[173] http://www.muslimsinamerica.org/
[174]
http://www.muslimsinamerica.org/index.php?option=com_content&task=view&id=12&Itemid=30

[175] **6:116.** And if you obey most of those upon the earth, they will mislead you from the way of Allah. They follow not except assumption, and they are not but falsifying.

[176] Sahih Muslim Hadith, **Hadith 270,** Narrated by **AbuHurayrah**

[177] 2:115. And to Allah belongs the east and the west. So wherever you [might] turn, there is the Face* of Allah. Indeed, Allah is all-Encompassing and Knowing. (*footnote to ayah 2:19: Allah states in the Qur'an that He has certain attributes such as hearing, sight, hands, face, mercy, anger, coming, encompassing, being above the Throne, etc. Yet, He has disassociated Himself from the limitations of human attributes or human imagination. Correct Islamic belief requires faith in the existence of these attributes as Allah has described them without applying to them any allegorical meanings or attempting to explain how a certain quality could be (while this is known only to Allah) and without comparing them to creation or denying that He (*subhanhu wa ta'ala*) would have such a quality. His attributes are befitting to Him
alone, and *"There is nothing like unto Him."* (42:11)

[178] **29:56**   O My servants who believe! truly spacious is My Earth: therefore serve ye Me (and Me alone)!

[179] Sunan of Abu-Dawood
Hadith 455   Narrated by
Aisha, Ummul Mu'minin

The Apostle of Allah (peace be upon him) commanded us to build mosques in different localities (i.e. in the locality of each tribe separately) and that they should be kept clean and be perfumed.

[180] 72:18. And [He revealed] that the masjids are for Allah, so do not invoke with Allah anyone.

[181] **2:143**. And thus We have made you a median [i.e., just] community that you will be witnesses over the people and the Messenger will be a witness over you

[182] The Arabic word translated "defilement" is Al-Rijsa [الرَّجْسَ], the root word is rajasa [رَجَسَ] and has root meanings of An abomination, punishment, indignation, doubt.
[183] A Dictionary and Glossary of the Qur'an, John Penrice, p. 91

[184] Ninety Nine Names of Allah, Muhammad iqbal Siddiqi, p. 41

[185] Ninety Nine Names of Allah, Muhammad iqbal Siddiqi, p. 42

[186] Ninety Nine Names of Allah, Muhammad iqbal Siddiqi, p. 43

[187] Ninety Nine Names of Allah, Muhammad iqbal Siddiqi, p. 124

[188] Ninety Nine Names of Allah, Muhammad iqbal Siddiqi, p. 104

[189] Dictionary of the Holy Qur'an, Abdul Mannan Omar, p. 444 - 445

[190] Dictionary of the Holy Qur'an, Abdul Mannan Omar, p. 105

[192]http://www.saylor.org/site/wp-content/uploads/2011/08/HIST351-2.3.2-Sharia.pdf, 1/21/12

[194] Ninety Nine Names of Allah, Muhammad iqbal Siddiqi, p. 62, 63

[195] Ninety Nine Names of Allah, Muhammad Iqbal Siddiqi, p. 84

[196] I departed from the Saheeh International translation on the term Wadudun (وَدُودٌ). "Most Loving is the translation of Wudud from Ibn Kathir. Yusuf Ali translates the term "Loving Kindness"

[197] Ninety Nine Names of Allah, Muhammad Iqbal Siddiqi, p. 31, 32

[198] Ninety Nine Names of Allah, Muhammad Iqbal Siddiqi, p. 130

[199] A Dictionary and Glossary of the Qur'an, John Penrice, p. 23

[200] An Arabic English Lexicon by Edward William Lane Part 1, p. 83

[201] Ninety Nine Names of Allah, Muhammad Iqbal Siddiqi, p. 23

[202] Anas reported: The Holy Prophet was on the saddle (of camel) with Mu'az behind him. He addressed thrice: O Mu'az! He replied "Present to thee, O Prophet, and fortune to thee!" He said: There is nobody bearing witness that there is no deity but Allah and Muhammad is the Apostle of Allah with sincere belief in his heart, but Allah has prohibited for him the Fire. He inquired: O Apostle of Allah, should I not deliver this to the people that they may seek good? He said: In that case, they will sit idle. Mu'az communicated this innocently at the time of his death. – Agreed

[203] A Dictionary and Glossary of the Qur'an, John Penrice, p. 46

[204] Dictionary of the Holy Qur'an, Abdul Mannan Omar, p. 19-D

[205] http://www.tyndalearchive.com/TABS/Lane/, 9/30/12

[206] http://www.tyndalearchive.com/TABS/Lane/, 9/30/12

[207] The Conservation Of Races, W.E. Burghardt Du Bois, 1897

[208] The Strivings of the Negro People, W.E. Burghardt Du Bois, 1897

[209] A Dictionary and Glossary of the Qur'an, John Penrice, p. 52

[210] http://en.wikipedia.org/wiki/Fana_(Sufism), 11/20/11

[211] The Ballot or the Bullet, Malcolm X, April 3, 1964, Cleveland, Ohio, http://www.edchange.org/multicultural/speeches/malcolm_x_ballot.html

[212] The Fire Next Time, James Baldwin, p 40 9 (carried forward from Islam and the Blackamerican, p. 25)

Negroes in this country -- and Negroes do not, strictly or legally speaking, exist in any other -- are taught really to despise themselves from the moment their eyes open on the world. This world is white and they are black. White people hold the power, which means that they are superior to blacks (intrinsically, that is: God decreed it so), and the world has innumerable ways of making this difference known and felt and feared.

Long before the Negro child perceives this difference, and even longer before he understands it, he has begun to react to it, he has begun to be controlled by it. Every effort made by the child's elders to prepare him for a fate from which they cannot protect him causes him secretly, in terror, to begin to wait, without knowing that he is doing so, his mysterious and inexorable punishment. He must be "good" not only in order to please his parents and not only to avoid being punished by them; behind their authority stands another, nameless and impersonal, infinitely harder to please, and bottomlessly cruel. And this filters into the child's [http://negroartist.com/writings/JAMES%20BALDWIN/The%20Fire%20Next%20Time.htm]

[213] Why We Can't Wait, Martin Luther King, Jr., p.23
[214] I do want to note that I do accept the possibility, through DNA testing to discover your tribe and to reconnect by developing a relationship with your people in the here and now.

[215] Muslims on the Americanization Path?, Edited by Yvonne Yazbeck Haddad, John L. Esposito, p. 267

[216] Islam and the Black American, Looking Toward the Third Resurrection, p. 49

[217] Identity and Destiny, The Formative Views of the Moorish Science Temple and the Nation of Islam, Ernest Allen Jr. , from Muslims on the Americanization Path?, Yvonne Yazbeck Haddad, John L. Esposito, p. 171

[218] Even in Difficult Times, a Self-Help Guru Finds a Willing and Paying Audience , ,http://www.nytimes.com/2009/03/08/nyregion/08riches.html,

[219] The title of this short piece acknowledges Black English. According to Michael Eric Dyson, black English grew out of the fierce linguisticality of black existence, the insistence by blacks of carving a speech of their own from the remnants of African languages and piercing and stitching those remnants together in the New World with extant patterns of English for the purpose of communication and survival. Source: Is Bill Cosby Right? (Or Has The Black Middle Class Lost Its Mind?), p. 72

30:22 And of His signs is the creation of the heavens and the earth and the diversity of your languages and your colors. Indeed in that are signs for those of knowledge.

[220] http://www.urbandictionary.com/define.php?term=hataz, 3/31/12

[221] Sahih Muslim Hadith, **Hadith 270,** Narrated by **AbuHurayrah**

OUR VISION

Our goal is to help you get your story into print. It really is that simple.

As authors ourselves, we understand the frustration of repeated rejections from the big publishing companies and the elitist agents. It becomes a Catch 22 when you have to be a big name in order to get published and become a big name. We're here to eliminate that step and the potential heartbreak that accompanies it and put the power back in your hands.

We are not a "vanity publisher" who charges you as much as $8,000 to receive a handful of substandard paperbacks, just so you can hand them out to the relatives at Christmas and never sell another copy. We get you published and marketed both in paperback and e-book format on Amazon.com and other major online retailers. We also don't charge to get you published, we only charge a small fee for preparing your book.

You earn up to a 60% royalty rate with us, instead of the typical 10% that the traditional publishing houses pay. Why should you do all the work and allow them to keep 90% of your profit? And the best part is, you retain 100% of the rights to your work!

THE FUTURE IS NOW!

Gone are the days when an author would sit in front of an old manual typewriter, rubbing holes in the paper or filling their office garbage cans with unsalvageable scrap. The publishing industry is evolving. The old publishing houses are becoming dinosaurs. E-books are everywhere. They are cheaper than old-fashioned books, use less paper and ink, faster to produce, take up less space and can be read on any computer, e-reader or smartphone.

Success comes to those who make opportunities happen, not those who wait for opportunities to happen. You can be successful too, you just have to try...

A recent poll suggested that nearly 85% of parents would encourage their child to read a book on an e-reader. More than 1 in 5 of us owns an e-reading device and the number is climbing rapidly. For every 100 hardcover books that Amazon sells, it sells 143 e-books. They also never go out of print!

Hundreds of thousands of indepedent authors, just like you, are selling their profitable work as you read this. E-book sales have grown over 200% in the past year and account for more than $1 billion in annual sales.

Chances are, you don't even know the difference between a PDF, mobi, ePub, doc, azw, or the fifteen other competing formats struggling to coexist on the sixteen types of e-reader devices such as the Kindle or the Nook. Even if you are able to keep up with all the devices and their formats, do you want to spend the money for expensive software to convert your files, or the many hours it will take to figure out how it works? Will you be able to create an interactive table of contents?

Our editors are professionals with experience in computer science, graphic design and publishing. We can do the work or you, creating a top-notch book that you will be proud of. Of course, you still have to write it, but that's the fun part...

BE A PART OF OUR COMMUNITY

Reach your intended audience in the worldwide marketplace by distributing your work on Amazon, Barnes and Noble and other major online booksellers. Earn royalties, get feedback, Join the discussions in the forum and meet other people in our community who share the same interests you do.

We will publish your fiction or non-fiction books about just about anything, including poetry, education, gardening, health, history, humor, law, medicine, pets, philosophy, political science, psychology, music, science, self-help travel, science-fiction, fantasy, mystery, thriller, children and young adult, etc....

http://www.starrynightpublishing.com

Made in the USA
Charleston, SC
22 December 2012